Remix and Life Hack in Hip Hop

YOUTH, MEDIA AND CULTURE SERIES

Volume 6

Series Editors

Shirley R. Steinberg, *University of Calgary; Director of Institute of Youth and Community Studies, University of the West of Scotland*
Awad Ibrahim, *University of Ottawa, Canada*

Editorial Board

Annette Coburn, *The University of the West of Scotland*
Giuliana Cucinelli, *Concordia University, Montreal, Canada*
Rhonda Hammer, *UCLA, USA*
Mark Helmsing, *Michigan State University, USA*
Brian Johnson, *Bloomburg University, PA, USA*

Scope

Taking the notion of critical youth studies, this series features top scholars in critical media and youth studies. Coupling edgy topics with a critical theoretical lens, volumes explore the impact of media and culture on youth … and the impact of youth on media and culture.

Remix and Life Hack in Hip Hop

Towards a Critical Pedagogy of Music

Michael B. MacDonald
MacEwan University, Canada

SENSE PUBLISHERS
ROTTERDAM/BOSTON/TAIPEI

A C.I.P. record for this book is available from the Library of Congress.

ISBN: 978-94-6300-498-5 (paperback)
ISBN: 978-94-6300-499-2 (hardback)
ISBN: 978-94-6300-500-5 (e-book)

Published by: Sense Publishers,
P.O. Box 21858,
3001 AW Rotterdam,
The Netherlands
https://www.sensepublishers.com/

All chapters in this book have undergone peer review.

The following book chapters are reprinted here with permission from the publishers:

Chapter 1: Aesthetic Systems Theory: Doing Hiphop Aesthetics Research Together. *MusiCultures. Journal of the Canadian Society for Traditional Music*, Community-engaged research special edition, 2015, pp. 34–53.

Chapter 3: Cultural Studies of Youth Culture: Aesthetics as Critical Aesthetics Education. In *Critical Youth Studies Reader*, Awad Ibrahim & Shirley R. Steinberg (Eds.), Peter Lang Publishing, New York, 2014, pp. 434–443.

Chapter 5: Hip-hop Citizens: Local Hip-Hop and the Production of Democratic Grassroots Change in Alberta. In *Hip-Hop(e): The Cultural Practice and Critical Pedagogy of International Hip-Hop*, Brad Porfilio and Michael J. Viola (Eds.), Peter Lang Publishing, New York, 2012, pp. 95–109.

Chapter 6: A Pedagogy of Cultural Sustainability: YEGH3 (Edmonton hip-hop history) as a Decentralized Model for Hip-hop's Global Microhistories. In *See You at the Crossroads: Hip Hop Scholarship at the intersections. Dialectical Harmony, Ethics, Aesthetics and Panoply of Voices*, Brad Porfilio, Debangshu Roychoudhury, and Lauren M. Gardner (Eds.), Sense Publishers, Rotterdam, 2014, pp. 29–44.

Chapter 8: Cipher5 as Method in Hiphop Kulture Research: Developing a Critical Community-Engaged Research Method for a Cultural Studies of Music. In *Research Methods for Critical Youth Studies*, Awad Ibrahim and Shirley R. Steinberg (Eds.), Peter Lang Publishing, New York, 2015.

Cover image by Andre Hamilton

Printed on acid-free paper

TABLE OF CONTENTS

Section II: Case Studies in Hiphop Kulture

ACKNOWLEDGEMENTS

My adventure in critical pedagogy would not nearly be as rich as it is without the constant support I receive from a global network of critical youth scholars, committed critical pedagogues, and the Edmonton Hip Hop community that has embraced both my ongoing research and me. A big thank you to all of you who inspire and challenge me, especially my community research partner Andre Hamilton aka Dre Pharoh.

A special and heartfelt thank you is necessary for my mentor Dr. Shirley Steinberg who is a constant support, guide, friend, and sister.

Some chapters were originally published and have been reprinted here with permission:

Aesthetic Systems Theory: Doing Hiphop Aesthetics Research Together. *MusiCultures. Journal of the Canadian Society for Traditional Music.* Community-engaged research special edition. 2015 (pp. 34–53).

Cipher5 as Method in Hiphop Kulture Research: Developing a Critical Community-Engaged Research Method for a Cultural Studies of Music. In *Research Methods for Critical Youth Studies.* Awad Ibrahim and Shirley R. Steinberg (eds.) Peter Lang Publishing, New York. 2015.

Cultural Studies of Youth Culture: Aesthetics as Critical Aesthetics Education. In *Critical Youth Studies Reader.* Awad Ibrahim and Shirley R. Steinberg (eds.) Peter Lang Publishing, New York. 2014 (pp. 434–443).

A Pedagogy of Cultural Sustainability: YEGH3 (Edmonton hip-hop history) as a Decentralized Model for Hip-hop's Global Microhistories. In *See You at the Crossroads: Hip Hop Scholarship at the intersections. Dialectical Harmony, Ethics, Aesthetics and Panoply of Voices.* Brad Porfilio, Debangshu Roychoudhury, and Lauren M. Gardner (eds.) Sense Publishers, Rotterdam. 2014 (pp. 29–44).

Hip-hop Citizens: Local Hip-Hop and the Production of Democratic Grassroots Change in Alberta. In *Hip-Hop(e): The Cultural Practice and Critical Pedagogy of International Hip-Hop.* Brad Porfilio and Michael J. Viola (eds.) Peter Lang Publishing, New York. 2012 (pp. 95–109).

To see Cipher5 in action please check out: my film *Megamorphesis: The Hip Hop Quest for Enlightenment* available to screen online at michaelbmacdonaldfilms.ca

INTRODUCTION

From Culture to the Production of Aesthetic Systems

Creativity is labour. It is the work that you do when you innovate with a set of resources. I will not say that it is a special form of labour, because I think it is very common. Creativity is a form of work that innovates and differentiates. Often it is said that creativity is making something from nothing. But this is an error. Creativity is the practice of innovating with a set of resources. It is true however, that sometimes the innovation produces a change in kind, a historic break from what was there before. Hiphop Kulture is precisely one of these examples. It did not emerge from a void, but from a set of technical and technological innovations using an existing set of aesthetic resources. This is not an attempt to undermine the incredible contribution to world culture that has been made by hip-hop music. But it does shift focus away from the creative capitalist heroes of the music industry, so that we might see more clearly the generations of youth who have used Hiphop Kulture to innovate upon themselves, to become something more, and to belong to something that was not there a moment ago. This is the core of *Remix and Life Hack*. Hiphop Kulture is NOT a music genre, it is MUCH more, and exploring how the sharing of aesthetic resources builds community, and how situated learning plays a necessary role in cultural sustainability draws out questions that may lead to a model of community located cultural education, and a starting point for a critical pedagogy of music.

Culture, it has been said, is the most difficult word in the English language to define.[1] The French philosopher Michel Foucault argued however, that *culture* could be understood as the administration of techniques and technologies of living. A culture is a set of practices, ways of doing things. He referred back to the Greek term techne, the root of technology and technique. He argued that culture is a word that signifies a set of techniques and technologies for constructing both the physical manifestations of a way of living but is also, and most importantly, the outward manifestation of an individual and group subjectivity. Wade Davis argued separately that losing a culture is like losing an old growth forest of the mind. So what is the impact of making a culture in a post or de-colonial context?

Colonization is the ideological and physical repression of *technologies* of expression (language, clothes, ritual) that disrupts *techniques* of subjectivity formation that erodes historical forms of sensibility. It is true to say that colonization wipes out culture, but this does little to explain how colonial practices interrupt the complex connections, the ecology of expressive practices and embedded knowledges that function as a factory for collective and individual subjectivity. This discussion is critical for educators who, by ignoring the often colonial location of arts pedagogy, risk the reification of culture that occurs when the location and practices of acculturation necessary for a social ecology are ignored for effective discipline and classroom management. Repeating the claim that culture is too difficult is an obfuscation that ensures that pedagogies that support local communities are not developed. And in extreme cases hides the damage done when there is a reification of aesthetic practices into "cultural objects" and counterfeit immersive touristic experiences. Saying 'culture is hard' is not an excuse to ignore the politics of cultural representation, the ongoing practice of colonization, and the political struggle youth cultures have been engaged in for generations. But where does this politics occur? I argue throughout that it is more than identity politics, although this is an important part. It is a politics of value(s) located in sensibility that requires a cultural studies of sensibility. A place to start? Take and remake aesthetics, and the aesthetic education it supports, from philosophers in the colonial European heritage. Replace it with a cultural studies of sensibility and a critical pedagogy of aesthetic systems.

WHY HIPHOP KULTURE?

Hiphop Kulture emerges from a history of African American innovation upon the production of urban subjectivity, a contribution of world changing importance that includes Sojourner Truth, W.E.B. DuBois, Back to Africa, the Harlem Renaissance, the Civil Rights Movement, the Black Panthers, funk, soul, Motown and many more lesser known innovations.[2] Creative urban youth laboured with accessible sound reproduction technology and built new ways of communication across visual, aural/oral, gestural, and textual channels. Their labour took shape into what we now call hip-hop music. The story of Hiphop Kulture is more than the big hits and world-wide dissemination of generations of styles. While the world is familiar with Jay-Z and Kanye West, many hiphoppas labour to sustain Hiphop Kulture in their communities far from the big stages, world tours, and hit singles enjoyed by a shockingly few American hiphoppas. For those few mega stars, their creative labour is calculated in billions of dollars. But for most hiphoppas, their creative labour may never get expressed in economic terms, but in social capital, in the production of collective and individual subjectivity, in the bonds of love that build and hold communities together, and in the healing of broken hearts, broken homes, and broken neighborhoods in broken cities.

But it is now increasingly difficult to separate the production of subjectivity from the market place. Karl Marx's notion of the social factory has moved center stage with the emergence of the creative industries. And with this move a counter move, a resistance to the commodification of everything is required.

SUBJECTIVITIES TRAPPED BY SYSTEMS OF GLOBAL CAPITAL

I am Michael. This simple sentence articulates three active forces, subject-subjectivity-identity, entwined in my aesthetics of self (Foucault). Michael is a white male heterosexual professor. Michael is constructed and is a construction. Musically,

I've never been comfortable with my whiteness. Not because I am musically white—not at all—I was not brought up in the classical music tradition. I was brought up in the gospel, soul, and blues traditions. My grandfather played traditional Cape Breton fiddle music and country blues and gospels on guitar. The whiteness that I understand, that I am comfortable with, is the whiteness that has not been included in Whiteness. It is a whiteness that I have difficulty articulating, and will therefore become the subject of another book. It is a whiteness that I only began to understand when I read Joe Kincheloe's work on blues epistemology, a subject I will circle back to a number of times in this book. There is no question however that I have been absorbed into the Whiteness of European colonization, the Whiteness of racial power, of a white-male-professor, the colonization of aesthetics. The power of Whiteness consumes subjectivities, encases and racializes sensibilities. I attempt to do two things in this book. The first is to turn against the history of Aesthetic philosophy, not by way of dismissal, but in an attempt to save the study of sensibility from European racialized, colonial philosophy. I believe there is much to be won by doing this. The second, is to locate a new study of aesthetics—as a philosophy of sensibility and community—in the local, thus undermining the attempted universality and life destroying critical objective distance built into European aesthetic philosophy. These philosophical and methodological acts become political for me because they inform my identity as Michael or Professor MacDonald. Michael the professor is being shaped by the social structures of the university, policed by the practice of European aesthetic philosophy, colonial philosophers and art critics. I, however am also shaping Michael, as a resistant philosopher, a researcher who builds healthy relationships, contributes to community, attempts to enact radical love against the power of Whiteness that is trying to consume me.

Before I went to graduate school I used to be Mike. When I was a kid in Cape Breton Nova Scotia I was sometimes Mick, sometimes Little Bar (my father's name is Barry). It was a strange process to introduce myself as Michael, I felt like an imposter. I was also aware that I was transitioning from artist/musician to graduate student and professor. A class transition was taking place that was also transforming my masculinity. My haircuts became more regular, I began wearing a shirt and tie without irony, buying the blazer with elbow patches, shaving everyday. I was making Michael within structures of power that were shaping Michael. Students played their role by treating me with "more respect" (more distance) the more I visually conformed to Whiteness. I began to accept that success—whatever that meant—was bound up in the successful shaping of Michael.

But it is not Michael who addresses you now, nor is it Michael that watches and reports. *I* am not Michael. Michael is a government sanctioned and supported identity, a label, a provable thing that governments and businesses enumerate, plan for, profit from. Michael is a label for a single locatable animal. And the animal that I am has lots of needs that I seek to satisfy. But I am not only this body I am also a consciousness, a subject, reaching out to you through print…even though I am no longer here. I was here. This is my proof. My tracing. Perhaps you will try to see me in a photo, try to feel the articulate consciousness that emerges entwined with the neural complexities and social-neural wiring that runs through the folded flesh hidden away in my skull. I am simultaneously Michael and not-Michael. I am a reflective consciousness that feels itself, tries to undersand what it means "to be" in a sea of senses, that sometimes feels separate from the body that it requires, that sometimes, for a moment, feels like it is suffocated by its materiality. Writing externalizes the I, my subject, and gets a little closer to you, your subject. I slip from my materiality, my subject free and liquid, for a moment pooling somewhere between Michael and my laptop, until I take shape on the screen. This process and liquid not-yet is subjectivity, an important theme in this book. I want to contribute to the liberation of aesthetics in the hopes that we can develop a critical pedagogy of sensibility. An aesthetic education that delves into the fluxes of sense and desire, that has as its subject, not a history of art works, but a history of human becoming. I hope you are reaching out as well. Maybe someday you will tell me about being moved by my words. We will have a moment to share:

> To write is to do other than announce oneself as an enclosed individual... To write, ... is to write to a stranger, to a friend... Friendship is always a political act, for it unites citizens into a polis, a (political) community... It is the difference between me and my friend that allows meaning. And it is meaning, the meaningfulness of the world, that is consciousness. (Kathy Acker *cited in* Braidotti, 2006, 144)

I don't know why I reach out. I am compelled to create, to make music, to make movies, to discover words, to make knowledge, to share connections. This energy is not the same as my subject nor identity. It is the *am* in I *AM* Michael. This is subjectivity, the verb form of subject, it is becoming. It is the production of subjectivity.

When I first started trying to get my head around my own subjectivity I imagined it to be a life energy that moved like an underground stream. Life energy was a flow and I was an individual expression of it, like an underground stream that emerges above ground through a crack in a rock. I liked the idea that I was an individual expression of creativity, a background energy of creativity that flows. This metaphor shows up quite a bit in thinking about creativity, as if creativity is a flow that is 'out there' that creative people can connect with. Creativity is often described as energy.

But I'm not a crack in a rock, and creativity is in fact not found 'out there' in any one place, from an external location to be tapped into. And there isn't inside either. There's no location of creativity; innovations emerge from the functioning of complex systems. Acts of differentiazation, of not being Michael, not being Mike, not being flesh, not being who I was the moment before I wrote this. Metaphors were in my way. My subjectivity emerges from my life energy, but not in a metaphysical way. It emerges complexly from biological, mental, social, and environmental systems. Humberto Maturana and Francisco Varela explain in "The Tree of

Knowledge" (1992) how, through autopoiesis and self-organization, consciousness emerges *from the materiality of the body*. Thoughts are both material and creative! We are stardust monsters! We now know (thanks to brain scans) that thoughts are electric constellations comprised of electric impulses traversing folds we call brain, fed by sensations of incoming data coupled with retained data (memory), or other connections, that shape perception. We are a constellation. Subjectivity emerges from this constellation we call consciousness, shaped by recursive operations that second-order cybernetics theorist Gregory Bateson explored in "Steps to an Ecology of Mind" (1972). Christopher Small, building on Bateson, argued that music contributes to the processes of social formation that he called musicking. Small argued that the noun form or the word *music* gets in the way of understanding what music really is; that music is not a noun but rather a verb and needs to be understood as musicking. The switch from music to musicking is not semantic but ontological. Musicking is an aesthetic system that produces. Aesthetic resources constitute the system.

Subjectivity seems to be shaped as we relate to our environment, in much the same way James J. Gibson (1979) called affordances:

> The affordances of the environment are what it offers the animal, what it provides or furnishes, either for good or ill…refers to both the environment and the animal in a way that implies the complementarily of the animal and the environment. (127)

One Sunday afternoon when I was very young I sat in the living room with my grandmother and parents listening to the radio. I was lost in the music and the warm sun that flooded the little room. My grandmother spoke to my parents saying, "Look at his foot, he is a musician". When I was a young boy I sometimes played piano during family parties. At one of these an uncle stood next to me and watched me play. In the middle of a song he said, "You need to keep playing as you get older, girls will kiss you for this".

In *The Republic* Plato warned that the state should be concerned about music education, and maybe he was correct. He argued that modes (scales) produce ways of feeling, that some modes produce contentment and others violence and war. Music stirs and motivates action. Music works on affect, on sensibility, as it works on our skin, our ears and our memories.

REMIX AND LIFE HACK

Remix and Life Hack explores the idea that people are affected by art, and further, that we remix aesthetic resources to self-produce. The idea of Life Hack is useful here because it implies, unlike education, that you use technology to make life easier; for instance, a life hack is using your car's seat warmer to keep the pizza warm on the drive home. I'm using it a little differently. I'm suggesting that we life hack our subjectivities by using the aesthetic resources available in our society. I'm further arguing, as I will over and over again in the collection of essays in this book, that

Hiphop Kulture needs to be understood in this way if we are going to understand its social and evolutionary significance.

I am one of many people that I have known for whom music is not just something one listens to but is a social technology for building, shaping, and changing oneself in concert with others. We use music and other aesthetic resources, like clothes, behaviors, and locations to resonate together. This understanding of music is difficult to locate in academic literature even though it is the foundational assumption of every New York glossy style magazine editorial board and every punk e-zine. If we are going to understand the role of art in our lives then we must take a different starting point, what I have called aesthetic systems theory.

This book is not about mainstream hip-hop. You might not know anything about Edmonton yet. We call it YEG after the airport call letters. These essays are a case study on the impact of Hiphop Kulture, as an example of the kinds of social changes that Hip Hop has made possible. Hiphop Kulture has emerged alongside changes in capitalism that must also be theorized. So while you may not know any of the artists in this book yet, and may not know anything about my city, I suspect that once you read these essays you will be able to apply our methods to your city. I hope this is a shout out to community-engaged researchers and activists concerned with autonomous culture and the impacts of capitalism. I am going to share with you our work here in Edmonton, not so that you know about Edmonton, but so that you can trace our methods and apply them. We have imagined a future where Hiphop Kulture (and all autonomous cultures) can imagine themselves as social constellations, networks, rhizomes, where neighborhoods and cities contribute nodes in a growing and developing global cultural system. It will be great if you can use this book to connect with us, visit us, and invite us to visit you. This is a shout out to the world of Hiphop Kulture, a global network that we know is out there but we don't yet know how to actively plug into.

My approach to the ethico-aesthetic politics of music culture begins with the realization that I have used music to build myself over and over again. And not just music, but the aesthetic resources associated with music culture. And I am not alone. I have been working with other people who have been doing the same. We get these aesthetic resources from media and inherit them from culture, and innovate some of them. It feels like I begin to see something swirling around and I connect with it, and use it to shift myself, learning something new about who I can be, what I might be. This is a long way from the rational subject who observes art at a distant and with a discerning, critical eye. This is a long way from bourgeois art galleries. We have no distance from art, dissolved by the industrial processes Walter Benjamin gave name to in his famous *Art in the Age of Mechanical Reproduction*. Sometime between the Jazz *hip cats* of the 1930s, the rise of urban life, the mass manufacturing of style, and the emergence of the Harlem Renaissance, the Beats, and succession of youth culture from rock and roll to hip-hop *aesthetics* and *life* became inseparable. But not only this: aesthetics *and ethics* and life. That self-aesthetic production has ethical and political registers and that these have provided a framework for political struggle into the 21st century is played out everywhere. We live within a system of aesthetic resources that we can no longer see the outside of. As writers in second-order cybernetics have argued:

> If reality is conceived as a cognitive construct, as an effect or correlate of observation, then descriptions of reality become descriptions of observation. When observation becomes an integral part of reality, it can no longer be understood as a kind of Archimedean Point—such as the one Descartes claimed to have found in his *Mediations*. There is no one place where all that is certainly real can be grounded. Observation loses its simplicity—an observer can no longer observe reality without taking into account its very observation as a generating element of reality. A constructivist view of reality directs the attention of observation of the observation of reality. It becomes second-order observation—and the theory of second-order observation is called second-order cybernetics. Second-order cybernetics is concerned with the reality-construction of observing systems. (Moeller, 2006, 71)

As I will explore in more detail, and from a number of critical directions throughout the text Kant looked at the art object in the 18th century, Walter Benjamin looked at the machines that mechanically reproduced art objects in the early 20th century, Howard Becker looked at the industrial processes that produced the artworld of the late 20th century, but now we can no longer objectify the system. I cannot see an outside. The machines of aesthetic reproduction swallow up life and our scholarship must chase this down the rabbit hole. I build myself with aesthetic resources that swirl around me, I build myself by observing others, when I am integrated within social groups, excluded from others, conscious of my body and trying to put all of this together. For an observer, the question is not whether or not my observations are *real* or *true* but whether or not there is consciousness of the impact of these forces at work. It is not enough for an observer to observe, but also to engage in a thoughtful, heartful observation, to ask what the implications will be if I choose to use these particular aesthetic resources as I build myself. It is no longer a discussion of observation and feeling but now also one of design. The observer is not distant of the system being observed but is a constituent of the system. As Joe Kincheloe (2005) has argued, it is necessary to move towards critical constructivism, to recognize that knowledge construction must also contend with forces of power. I would like to push this further, to see subjectivity as a construction.

TOWARDS A CRITICAL PEDAGOGY OF MUSIC

In critical youth media education practice, it is necessary to theorize along with students the forces of aesthetic governmentality (domination) and techniques of aesthetic subjectivation (formation of subjectivity) that form the ethico-aesthetic strata I call *aesthetic systems*. I take aesthetics to be the study of the field of communication resources used in expressive practices that contribute to the shaping of a field of *self and society*. These forces are emerging from the ongoing information revolution, emergent communication technologies, along with techniques of culture and the dominating techno-hegemonic force called hyperreality (Baudrillard). The domination of media culture and the minimum preparation of students for critical analysis of hyperreality has left the accompanying social transformations unchecked. Specifically, this analysis must focus on the capitalist mutations that expand production, exchange, and consumption of products to include the production of collective and individual subjectivities. Gary Genosko (2012), writing about Jean Baudrillard, said "welcome to the machine…ideology is embedded in the social relations [that] the forms of media dictate and induce. Media are thoroughly ideological" (76). Cognitive capitalism "produces and domesticates the living on a scale never before seen" (Boutang, 2011, 48) not eliminating material industrial production but reorganizing, remodeling, and incorporating the production of *subjectivity* under the rubrics of *financialisation*. We are products of the machinic assemblages of semiocapitalism, said Felix Guattari and Franco Berardi and we "emphasize that entire circuits and overlapping and communicating assemblages integrate cognitive labour and the capitalistic exploitation of its content" (Genosko, 2012, 150) where "the mind, language and creativity [are the] primary tools for the production of value" (Berardi, 2009, 21). This emergence of *semiocapitalism* requires a new theorization of the production of subjectivity, subject and identity within aesthetic systems. As semiocapitalism incorporates life within the production of value, it transforms social relationships in two observable ways, by: (a) transforming schools in the image of neoliberalism (see Henry Giroux) and (b) transforming anthropological culture into market culture. It is this second aspect that I want to examine because it is here where contemporary political action may be located, in either a resistance to market culture, or alternatively, community economic development within market culture.

My research begins with the premise that theories of resistance have tended towards dismissing the cultural industries (Adorno), but that successful movements have emerged from liberated spaces, zones of autonomous cultural production within the creative marketplace. For instance, a critical historiography of resistant youth culture would illustrate that aesthetic governmentality within hyperreality has been challenged over and over again by youth aesthetic movements. Whether it is folk, rock, punk, or Hiphop these aesthetic movements are guerrilla incursions into urban youth sensibility. Youth are innovating upon technologies and techniques of the manipulation of sensibility for the construction of new forms of individual and collective subjectivity. When we say youth culture—this is what we are really saying, and this lesson must be used against the hegemony of European aesthetic philosophy that continues to exclude. The implications of this exclusion are not just issues of funding, grants, and government support of youth artists, but also exclusion of subject areas from schools. Globally students are still learning more about Shakespeare, Mozart and Beethoven then they are the poets, musicians, and playwrights that live and work in their communities. Why are we not working with youth to critically develop a practical philosophy of sensibility? There are some examples of how schools support the development of local creativity, but these examples are few. But in just about any town you will find young people engaged in practical aesthetic philosophy, but you will rarely find their words in books.

This collection of essays is drawn from four years of community-engaged research in Hiphop Kulture in Edmonton, Alberta. Along the way, as a testament to community-engaged research, we have developed innovative methods of inquiry, methods of historiography, and methods of community media studies. *Remix and Life Hack* contributes to critical studies of media culture by adding a community-engaged research framework but also by informing this practice with Foucault's later theoretical work on subjectification and the aesthetics of self, Deleuze and Guattari's nomadic theories of subjectivity, Guattari's theories of machinic enslavement, and all organized around Paulo Freire's *culture circle*.

My interest in public aesthetics education arises from the transformation of globalizing network that are rocked by waves of social, cultural, economic and environmental crises. With only few exceptions, student learning is informed by what scholarly siloes deem to be important and not by the need to develop capacities to respond to a world in crisis. When we talk about the crises we are facing it is important not to abstract it, to mystify it and blame it on "the market". As folk singer and labour activist Utah Phillips was fond of saying, "The earth is not dying, it is being killed, and those who are killing it have names and addresses." We are working on developing a language to challenge rogue or *Zombie Capitalism* (Harman, 2010). For streams of cultural studies inspired by the Frankfurt School the study of the social, cultural, and psychological impacts of the emergence of capitalism are not new. Marx made many observations in the early days of industrial capitalism that are still relevant today. As we move through postindustrial capitalism into financial capitalism and the emerging semiocapitalism, or whatever it will be called, many systems of exclusion and inequality have only grown more intense, and certainly more global.[3] These emergent systems are impacting sensibility.

And though we have known for some time that this system damages we seem unable to make any significant change. Before cultural studies emerged, philosophers were already troubling over the fact that voters and workers would actively make decisions that were against their own interests. How does this happen? The theory of ideology was proposed and explored in a variety of interesting ways. From Marxist scholarship to the work that poststructuralists undertook to bring, as Deleuze and Guattari did in *Anti-Oedipus* and *A Thousand Plateaus*, to bring Marx and Freud together.

But if we look elsewhere we find praxis, where street based critical theory emerges from and is supported by action. Hiphop Kulture for instance, encouraged autonomy and a practice of thoughtful self-creation. In these essays I attempt to do three things at the same time: (a) replace European aesthetic philosophy with a new study of sensibility; (b) discuss Hiphop Kulture as an aesthetic system that opens new lines of inquiry into the relationship between subjectivity, sensibility, media and local urban spaces; and (c) locate public aesthetics education as a practice that supports local culture, defined as the sustainable reproduction of techniques of aesthetic production. These three points move towards complexification of music studies and music education philosophy *towards a critical pedagogy of music.*

NOTES

[1] Discussion about culture in cultural studies.
[2] In particular the cooperative economic innovations that have only recently been published.
[3] http://www.hup.harvard.edu/catalog.php?isbn=9780674504806

SECTION I

AESTHETIC SYSTEMS THEORY FOR A CRITICAL PEDAGOGY OF POPULAR MUSIC

AESTHETIC SYSTEMS THEORY[1]

Doing Hip Hop Research Together at Cipher5

INTRODUCTION[2]

Aesthetic education is involved in the production of subjectivity. From Plato (2000), to Matthew Arnold (1932), to Theodor Adorno (1977, 1991), it has been understood that youth are moulded by cultural education. Plato encouraged art education that would influence the development of youth taste in ways that would support the state. Arnold worried about the loss of high culture with the rise of cultural industries, and Adorno worried popular culture produced by cultural industries threatened to transform people into empty-headed consumers. These thinkers were all concerned about the relationship between aesthetic education and the formation of a "proper" subjectivity.

From the earliest theorizations of aesthetics and aesthetic education, the production of a "proper" subjectivity was key. Frederick Schiller argues that by learning to understand beauty, the "handmaid of pure intellectual culture" (1954, 11), morality and consciousness develop. From the 1950s to the 1980s, Canadian music education was guided by this humanist philosophy of aesthetic education (Wasiak, 2013, 29). It has since been argued that aesthetics has an overly narrow focus on the "musical work" (McCarthy & Goble, 2002), does not include a multiplicity of musical practices (Regelski, 1996), cannot be inclusive (Bowman, 1993), and that "a truly musical experience is not aesthetic in its nature or value" (Elliot, 1995, 125). Feeling that aesthetic education was too philosophical, critics have offered an action-based (or "praxial") music education philosophy that is "thriving in music education circles despite wishful thinking to the contrary by its detractors" (Regelski, 2011, 61). Heidi Westerlund however, while recognizing praxialism as a highly relevant approach, has suggested that "a reconstruction of the aesthetic may be possible without losing the important perspective of music as praxis" (2003, 46).

Unlike Westerlund, I do not think it is necessary or advisable to reach back to humanist aesthetics in music education. At the same time, I disagree with Regelski that "aesthetic speculations and abstractions are simply not needed to account for music's obvious affective appeal and for its manifold paraxial functions" (2011, 72). There is more to music performance than the playing of notes, and it is a history of experiences with these features that led to the creation of aesthetics in the first place. The way forward is a re-theorization of aesthetic theory and this redefinition need not be radical. A suitable aesthetic theory only requires acknowledging something that has been asserted since Plato: that the production of subjectivity and the production of art are intertwined in aesthetic education.

Praxialists argue that performing music is enough for music education, but it seems unlikely that only the performance of notes occurs during the performance of school music. It is necessary to point out here that praxialists forward their argument without recognizing the significance of the school music program as the context of music production. Praxialists treat the context of music performance unproblematically as if the music school is not already a cultural field into which music students are enculturated. While I agree with the praxialist critique of humanist aesthetics, I believe that there are still questions about aesthetic education that need to be answered. My concern is that ignoring or dismissing aesthetics risks obscuring educational processes, risks an anti-intellectualism in art production and obstructs theoretical pathways to our understanding of the function of symbolic systems in the formation of social groups and individuals.

In response to these concerns, I am developing a theory of aesthetic systems as an attempt to explain how music performance is an educational process that uses aesthetic resources to produce art objects and that through the making, sharing and using of artworks, group and individual subjectivities are produced. Aesthetic Systems Theory (AST) begins with the assumption that there are no uneducated musicians, but many unschooled ones. Through the study of music learning processes (both in and out of formal schools), researchers might access the dense systems of knowledge production that create aesthetics systems. The term "aesthetic systems" can be understood within a local traditional music community, a small and newly developing experimental group or a contemporary global musical movement like Hip Hop. "Aesthetic Systems" (AS), however, is not synonymous with genre, although genre may be an expression of AS within a capitalist system. AS is also not synonymous with culture. It is instead a theory of how aesthetic resources are used to produce a single system within complex systems we call culture. I propose AST as an approach to the cultural study of music. My formulation of AST emerges from cultural studies, critical pedagogy and the ethico-aesthetics of Felix Guattari.

AST attempts to explain how, through the use of aesthetic resources, group and individual subjectivities are produced. It is therefore necessary to explain what I mean by subjectivities. I follow Felix Guattari who proposed *the production of subjectivity* in contrast to the philosophical and humanities *subject*. The subject, according to Guattari (2008), is treated as if it were a consequence of human nature, itself a consequence of the biological body. Subjectivity, he agues, is not produced through language use the way structuralists asserted, but is instead "manufactured just as energy, electricity, and aluminum are" (2008, 47). Individual subjectivities are produced at the "intersection of determinations of various kinds, not only social but economic, technologic, the media and so on" (Guattari, 2008, 48). Instead of aesthetics being used to develop a given subject in the way Schiller imagined, to lead a subject from "baser" nature (sensuous) to "higher" moral and critical nature, Guattari's notion of the production of subjectivities highlights process. He suggests that there is no reason to assume a subject as *tabula rasa* when it is evident that we are all born into an already existing complex social network through which we are moulded. Like Adorno, who argued that people are produced by culture industries, Guattari acknowledges the influence of group subjectivity, but unlike Adorno, Guattari argues that, through creativity, individual subjectivities emerge and complexify group subjectivity.

AST is about explaining how group subjectivities are produced through the making, sharing and using of aesthetic resources, and that within these group subjectivities and through the use of aesthetic resources, individual subjectivities *can* form. In traditional societies, this means local practices produce collective subjectivities sometimes called ethnicities, and that individual practices within this larger system leads to individual subjectivities. Global urban capitalist systems transform making, sharing and using into producing, exchanging and consuming. The work of global capitalist entertainment can be understood as producing collective subjectivities through the marketplace of aesthetic products and the art world (Becker, 1982). Guattari argues that it is necessary to understand how the introduction of global capitalism, what he calls "Integrated World Capitalism" (IWC) (2008, 53), changes the production of collective subjectivities, and the ways that consumption necessarily follows. If the formation of subjectivities requires aesthetic resources, but these resources are always products of mass consumption, how is any group subjectivity not always bound up with IWC? Guattari suggests the formation of liberated group subjectivities requires a micro-political move against mass production of IWC. This occurs in the localization of the production of subjectivities that Guattari calls "molecular revolutions" (2008: 61). This approach has been incorporated into cultural studies as *mediation* (Grossberg, 2010, 191).

Mediation is the point at which aesthetics and language, geographic, educational, political, social, sexual, economic systems intersect in the production of group and individual subjectivities. Understanding mediation requires community-engaged research that is capable of identifying key moments of mediation, or what Guattari calls "singularities." Singularities are sometimes mapped when members of a community join together in critical dialogue to share narratives of mediation. I have developed a research method for AST that draws upon Paulo Freire's culture circle (2010). I have used the culture circle method to study Hip Hop as an aesthetic system, with special attention on the production of Hiphop Kulture[3] (a collective subjectivity) and hiphoppas (individual subjectivities) in a community-engaged research project called Cipher5.

A cypher is a Hiphop circle most often associated with Emcees or b-boys/b-girls but there are DJ cyphers as well.[4] For Emcees, the cypher is a space to deliver freestyles (improvised rhyme over a beat) or to drop writtens (deliver pre-written rhymes) around the circle. But cypher can also refer to stream-of-consciousness delivery in rhyme. This kind of freestyle flow, something I have previously called "epistemological flow" (MacDonald, 2012), is often taken as a sign of mastery of emceeing. Cipher, spelled with an *i*, refers to processes of encryption and decryption.

In this sense, a *cipher* is a space where it is possible to deconstruct the production of subjectivity in a knowledge circle. The "five" in Cipher5 refers to knowledge as the fifth element of Hiphop Kulture after emceeing, graffiti, b-boying/b-girling, and DJing. Cipher5 is a cypher that brings together hiphoppas, students and professional researchers to produce and share knowledge about Hiphop Kulture. Cipher5 meets every Tuesday night at 7:00 pm at a local community centre. Participants and facilitators organize chairs in a circle (a cipher) and use the sound system, projector and computer for sharing videos, songs and other online content related to Hiphop Kulture.

My research into the learning processes in Hiphop Kulture developed from what I perceived to be a lack of cultural studies in music education research. It was as if, on the one hand, music schools had no culture and, on the other, that music cultures in "the street" had no educational strategies. I was interested in showing that aesthetic systems like Hip Hop produce subjectivities, using learning processes to do so. I hypothesized that if learning practices can be shown to produce subjectivities, then it is possible to respond to praxialists who imply that music schools do not have aesthetic systems. They certainly don't explain how these systems contribute to the production of student subjectivity. They do not acknowledge that aesthetic education produces subjectivity, and that school music might therefore be a place to produce experimental collective subjectivities that can be of benefit to the local community.

This chapter illustrates the way in which a community-engaged research practice can highlight the relationship between a music culture and the production of subjectivities. The starting assumption is that youth are already fully engaged in culture, and that in a democracy we do not need to follow the humanist aesthetics approach of instilling culture in our students from positions of power, but instead provide teachers and students with opportunities and capacities to make decisions about their participation in culture and the role it plays in the production of their group and individual subjectivities. Instead of making aesthetic decisions for youth, or obscuring the existence of aesthetics, we might instead develop an approach to art education that is a 'critical' study of aesthetic systems. I believe this will lead to the type of music education many profess to want, one devoted to the development of healthy group subjectivities engaged in critical consciousness or, in Paulo Freire's word, *conscientização* (2000).

Conscientização "can be literally translated as the process used to raise somebody's awareness" (Cruz, 2013: 171). It is, however, richer than this; it is

> the process in which men [and women], not as recipients, but as knowing subjects, achieve a deepening awareness both of the sociocultural reality that shapes their lives and of their capacity to transform that reality. (Freire, 1985: 93)

Conscientização is liberatory. Through critical education, subjects free themselves from an oppressor-oppressed dialectic that Hegel formulated as a master-slave narrative (Blunden, 2013, 11–28). They are able to do this, Freire theorizes, because they are capable of identifying social forces Gramsci called hegemony (Mayo, 2013, 53–64) and overcoming a built-in fear of freedom (Lake & Dagostino, 2013, 101–126). Like Schiller, Freire takes the student to be a humanist subject that is born into oppression. Unlike Schiller, however, Freire was working with actual oppressed indigenous people in Brazil. I am building on Freire's notion of conscientização, a critical consciousness that has to be built through community dialogue. But unlike Freire, I am arguing that conscientização is the critical production of group subjectivity.

I will leave whether or not our students are oppressed by universities or the cultural industries to another discussion. In this chapter, I will address the way Hip Hop aesthetic systems produce a Hip Hop subjectivity. To do this, I will propose a dialogic, community-engaged research method for aesthetic systems research that has been developed with members of the Edmonton hip-hop community.[5]

MULTI-DIMENSIONAL CARTOGRAPHY OF AESTHETIC SYSTEMS

This article attempts to unfold many levels of aesthetic systems, and will continue by introducing a community-based dialogical research method for aesthetic systems modeled on the dialogical approach used in the famous Keil-Feld dialogues in *Music Grooves* (1994). Keil and Feld use transcribed dialogues as an attempt at producing a transparent and experimental knowledge production technique. This is a form of cartography, a kind of mapping. They built their method on Mikhail M. Bakhtin's notions of dialogue, heteroglossia and multivocality, and on a secondary literature drawing from a broad list of disciplines (Keil & Feld, 1994, 13–14). Although I use this method, I have a different starting point: Paulo Freire's dialogic education (2005, 87–124). Dialogue is "the encounter between [people], mediated by the world, in order to name the world" (86) and dialogue cannot occur between "those who deny others the right to speak their word and those whose right to speak has been denied them" (ibid.). It must be noted that Keil and Feld's dialogue is between peers. Their exchange is famous because of the risks they took in moving outside of conventional academic method, providing new approaches but not necessarily accounting for the power differentials between the actors. I am taking a different approach. Following Freire, I am trying to create a cartographic technique within academic literature where those who are authorized to speak (Michael-as-professor), and those who are not (Andre-as-hiphoppa-community-member), can enter into dialogue with readers. This is not without challenges. For one, I realize that my position as a white, male professor, regardless of my personal history, might hide power inequalities even from me, and this might lead to mistakes and assumptions on my part.

Power dynamics are difficult to spot. For instance, Keil and Feld do not justify the significance of their dialogue. They are both recognized scholars and experimenters, and as such their dialogic performance may stand uncontextualized as radical scholarship. And, in fact, this scholarly performance earned them a great deal of cultural capital. Andre and I are not Keil and Feld, so I have contextualized our dialogue under the heading *Context*, which is followed by a conversation in the next section. Throughout the dialogue, Andre and I discuss our distinct perspectives and histories, and our motivations for the creation of Cipher5.

The inclusion of dialogue in this article layers information and methodology. This account offers a way of mapping flows between research partners that provides space for histories, subjectivities, methodologies and community. Cipher5 is both a research method and a community activity, and has both research and educational components. Andre and I are learning and sharing different things in different ways. I'm learning about Hiphop Kulture and research methods and Andre is learning about community organizing and university-community relations. We are learning about each other and ourselves. We are also learning how to navigate institutional structures, power relations, research dynamics and approaches to social knowledge formation. At the same time, we are clear about the educational mission we share: working to create an environment for the development of critical consciousness about Edmonton, one that makes visible the city's social forces, racial divides, economic realities and socio-cultural challenges. Freire used dialogic teaching in culture circles for the production of critical consciousness. Andre and I have found that the longer people sit in the circle, the more critically aware we become about how inseparable we are from our aesthetics.

DIALOGIC RESEARCH: CONTEXT

A significant step in the development of aesthetic systems theory was my reading of Paulo Freire's *Education for Critical Consciousness* (2010). Freire was working in literacy education with indigenous communities in Brazil when he came to recognize that he was stuck in an impossible situation. On the one hand, Brazil's industrialization meant increased opportunities for many indigenous Brazilians. On the other hand, participation in industrialization required being literate in Portuguese. Literacy education, in this case, contributed to an ongoing history of colonialism. Instead of choosing between teaching literacy or not, he developed a model of politically informed literacy education called critical pedagogy. Freire's principle was that you can teach something in a way that empowers learners. His hope was that critical pedagogy would allow learners to develop Portuguese literacy while seeing it as a cultural technology that is different from, but no better than, their own cultural technologies. When I was reading this, I saw similarities between the industrialization of Brazil and the globalization of cultural production. I asked myself whether I, as a music professor, could develop a pedagogical practice that acknowledges the global music industry while also respecting the locality of culture. I wanted a critical pedagogy of music to follow in Freire's footsteps. I leaned heavily on Freire's assertion that "the starting point for organizing the program content of education or political action must be the present, existential, concrete situation, reflecting the aspirations of the people" (2010, 95).

I created a university course about hip-hop culture, and with in-class support from Andre Hamilton, an Edmonton Hiphop cultural specialist, we began to discuss how to do ethical research on local Hip Hop. We read Linda Tuhiwai Smith's *Decolonizing Methodologies* (2012). Being in the classroom together revealed many shared interests, but we were also very different from one another. I grew up white in Cape Breton with Scottish Gaelic ancestry, while Andre grew up black in Edmonton with Jamaican ancestry. And yet there were similarities: we both grew up in Canada in small indie music markets that underwent exciting developments in the 1990s.

During the course, Andre introduced me to KRS-ONE's *The Gospel of Hip Hop* (2009), which I read over the semester. On the last day of class, Andre suggested keeping our conversation going. Andre came up with the idea of Cipher5 as a knowledge circle that could use *The Gospel of Hip Hop* as a central text. Over the next two years, we meet weekly with a growing number of hiphoppas and music student researchers. Over this time, I began to develop AST as a way of explaining the relationship between the production of subjectivity and the production of Hip Hop. *The Gospel of Hip Hop* led to the creation of the Temple of Hip Hop (TOHH) in New York City, and the creation of chapters across the United States and a few elsewhere in the world. In Edmonton, Cipher5 led to a Hip Hop symposium in the spring of 2014 at which members of the TOHH were invited to give presentations. Following the symposium, Cipher5 was nominated to become the Temple of Hip Hop Canada, with Andre, my co-facilitator, named as its director. The following conversation between me and Andre took place soon after Cipher5 was acknowledged by TOHH NYC as TOHH Canada. We felt that we needed to explore the way Cipher5 had come into being, the way our work had become a focal point for our community energy and how, through a series of events, we were now part of a growing global Hip Hop network. Andre and I met at my SoundCulturesLab at MacEwan University on February 10th and 13th 2012, and set up a recording device that was monitored by research assistants (RA) Diana Pearson and Roya Yazdanmehr, who later transcribed the conversation. I selected a section of the transcription for this paper. Sometimes Andre or I would begin to address the RAs to bring them up-to-date in the conversation, or to explain something that they didn't know. I wanted the RAs present for precisely this reason: so that we could create a reflective process. The transcription follows, edited slightly to read as I had originally intended: a conversation between me and Andre. The RAs were not addressed directly but the self-histories were given for their benefit, and ultimately for the benefit of readers. It was interesting for me to discover new things about Andre's history, and ultimately an alternative history of Cipher5, during this conversation. When I began the dialogue, I thought that my description covered both of us, but it turned out not to be so. Andre presented another version. Neither version is incorrect, and both are accurate. The dialogic exchange provided access to the multiplicities of mediation.

CHAPTER 1

DIALOGIC EXCHANGE

Andre

The Cipher has always been something of a natural formation in Hip Hop Culture. When I go back to the early-to-mid-80s when I was just basically a kid, 10, 11, 12 years old, [that's when] hip-hop really began for me. Don't get me wrong—Hiphop Kulture had been around for ten years before I discovered it. They said it started the year I was born.

I had some catching up to do, Edmonton being so displaced from New York, it took until '83 to come to fruition here. But breakdancing started after the Michael Jackson incident. Seeing that Michael Jackson had trained with a Los Angeles breakdancer and getting him up-to-speed on the hip new dancing that was started in America. What happened was on one of the Motown specials in 1983, when he debuted the *Thriller* album, he did a moonwalk across the stage and it just ROCKED the world! This one move ... it delivered *the culture* to Edmonton.

All of a sudden, every mall was having big breakdance competitions, especially Londonderry [a mall in North Edmonton] for some reason. It was always at Londonderry or some Northside mall where they would have these huge competitions, I mean 2000 kids trying to get in. If you weren't there three hours before the competition would start, you would never ever be able to see any performers. But naturally, cyphers would start forming around breakdancers. Even if people started spontaneously dancing, the cypher was always present. So it was a physical formation that seemed to be inherent with the culture, right from the start.

Cipher5 ... you have to understand that when I started my journey into Hiphop Kulture, and studying it, I didn't see any academic value. It was only after I met you, Michael, that I saw any academic value to what I was doing. But I *had* realized that I was a teacher. I had a certain kind of privilege, I had the support of my mother, and this is significant because I found myself in a situation where I knew I needed to be an MC. And in order to be an MC, I needed to teach myself a lot of stuff ... quick. So I knew that I needed to become a musician, I needed to become an engineer, my own booking agent and manager, I had to conceptualize something fresh, new and relevant and I had to become a master of the English language. I had to do it pretty fast because I wanted it bad. So there were these areas that I needed to master, not just be proficient at—to be awesome at—in order to excel as an MC, as a "HipHopicist." There was no community of Hip Hop businessmen, Hip Hop producers, lyricists, DJs, there was no community. All I could do was look at what was coming out of New York in the mid-'80s and match it. I had to sit down for a couple months and really get my head around, "How am I going to pull this off?" So I had to teach myself English, okay? Good English. So I started by reading the dictionary and studying the rhyming dictionary that I found at a Cole's bookshop—like a gift from God—one day! I'm like, "A rhyming dictionary!?" I couldn't believe it ... I'm like, "Yeahhhh," you know? It was just my bible; I read it for all of grade 8 and half of grade 9.

I really became fascinated with people who were masters of the English language. So I found myself really drawn to law shows, and watching lawyers, studying lawyers in court, and how they just mesmerized judges and crowds. I found myself reciting and kind of performing music that was already coming out. So I was really good at listening to a verse and being able to just like, press pause, and memorize stuff really fast, which made me really good in school. All the memorization that was going on with all the hip-hop songs I was trying to learn made me really good at cramming for tests, and is actually probably the reason I got through school the way I did.

A cypher in my basement became a safe haven, a school, a research labouratory, sometimes it felt like a prison. It became a lot of things, and my mother let me just do my thing. My father was an internationally recognized reggae musician who was touring around with Peter Tosh and Bob Marley, so that was a mixed blessing because she understood the need to just let me go downstairs and do my music and to be left to just do my thing. But it was a mixed blessing because after a certain amount of time being a musician, she really pushed the whole "Plan B" thing, which didn't help me much. It distracted me and made me doubt myself, you know? But there was a five-year period where I just stayed downstairs and taught myself how to master the English language, and how to produce music that was relevant, exciting and new. How to manage myself, how to compose, how to arrange, how to sell my music to local DJs, how to be able to call big corporate record companies and hustle phone calls until I was talking to A&R directors from all kinds of different labels. It taught me a lot of things, and how to manage myself, how to create this persona called Point Blank at the time.

This was completely solo. My younger brother was watching closely, but never claimed to be a Hip Hop artist. This was happening, just myself in the basement. What had happened was when I decided to announce that I was an MC, I announced it to a girl who happened to have a locker next to me in grade 10. I'm just like, "You know what? I'm an MC!" and she's like, "really?" And I'm like, "Yeah. I'm an MC. Straight up!" I made this proclamation to her because she had a locker right next to me. Her name was Nicki Rodney. What had happened is, two weeks after I made that proclamation, I get this phone call from Nicki Rodney and she says, "You said you're an MC, right?" And I was like, "Yeah," and a man took the phone and he says "Listen, I'm Bailey and I'm bringing Ice T and the Rhyme Syndicate to Edmonton. Would you like to be their opening act and tour with them?" I was stunned. I mean, I actually whited out … one of those defining moments in your life when you just see white. I accepted, but I had no real idea of what I was accepting 'cause I'd never really seen that many hip-hop shows anyways at that point. I didn't know what was expected of me; I didn't know what I was getting myself into. But I had three months to make it happen.

After I successfully rocked that show, something happened … my peers all over the city, you know, 3500 kids just like me, saw me doing it. And what that did for them is made them realize, "I can do it too!" which ignited a fire that just raged. So what ended up happening is, on a weekly basis—every weekend—I would have five, ten, fifteen kids from God knows where, some of them would even come from other towns to ask if I would teach them. Or, "How can I do this? How do you do this? How do you do that? How did you do this-that-and-the-next?" And that was a responsibility I took extremely seriously, to educate my generation on how to do what I was doing so that I wasn't alone, because it was a lonely life. It was just me doing it, and sure, I got off on it because I was the only one opening for every hip-hop act that ever came through Alberta for close to a decade.

So what ended up happening, I became a teacher. I was teaching my peers on all aspects of what I was doing. 182nd street [where I lived] was kind of a shady street, because we had six Edmonton housing project complexes all on this three-kilometre circular loop. With project living comes project thinking and lots of trouble. So I found myself grabbing kids who had creative potential, who were disciplined in school or in some other area of their lives. Maybe they were pursuing athletics or doing something besides sitting around, and I would pull them into my basement and give them opportunity. In addition, I had a lot of people approach me about … "apprenticeship"—I'm gonna call it that for the sake of this conversation—but I really had to intuitively filter out who needed to be there and who didn't. I feel good about the choices I made, because the people I took on went on to do some pretty great things.

So Cipher5 was a natural part of Hiphop Kulture, and it also came from a need to transcend our conditions on 182nd street, and it came from my own sense of responsibility to my peers and to the community. I've always felt a tremendous sense of responsibility to push us forward, and when I say us, I mean *earth*, and in my way, in a way I could. So I spent just as much time teaching as I did working on my own projects. So it was possible for me to take care of my own interests and still take care of my responsibility to my generation. So, this is where Cipher5 started.

Michael

There is something that I think needs to be clarified. You say Cipher5 started in your basement many years ago and that contradicts what I say about Cipher5 being started by us in our joint classroom experiment. And we've talked about this, that Cipher5 is both a practice and a thing. The group that we call Cipher5 is like the institutionalization—even though it's in a coffee shop—of what you were doing in your basement. We get together in a circle, a cypher, we read parts of the book collectively, we listen to music, discuss lyrics, sometimes write our own. We discuss graffiti, we talk about what's been released recently and talk to younger members about our experiences hearing something for the first time and doing something for the first time. We also learn from younger members what they think is hip and the kinds of techniques they are learning now, and how. Like how they are learning through YouTube and how they are exchanging beats with people all over the world.

Andre

Yeah, and this is a continuation. So, I was very pleased to see what Marlin [Politic Live] had been doing over the years because I kinda went off to do other things and Marlin really kinda carried the torch for a bit, y'know Marlin and Touch carried the 182 torch and kept that mentorship of others and this cycle of giving continued, so we're always very, very proud of his accomplishments. Then I saw Marlin was involved in a couple of research projects with *See Magazine* and doing some academic work.

He approached me about a research project that a professor was doing and that there was actually a Hiphop Kulture class that was gonna be happening at the U of A and this was, I was, was I in Vancouver at the time? I don't know where I was, I just remember being extremely excited that this was taking place and fascinated with who this teacher was. So, finally Marlin put us in touch and we were just going back and forth mutually expressing our interests of meeting, but it was three or four months that went by until we could actually get in the same room.

Michael, you invited me to come and just chill out and watch your class, so I went and I just ... I became fascinated, because here's this guy teaching hip-hop at U of A and that was ... that was monumental for me. It was monumental because I felt like our culture had finally made it somewhere other than a radio station or a MuchMusic control room; that we were being seen for something, for our ingenuity, the genius of it, the intelligence, rather than just as a moneymaker. It was this de-commodification to me, and don't get me wrong, there's intellectual exploitation that happens with all things, but in the moment it was different, it was a different kind of commodification, somethin' I was okay with, y'know.

Towards the end of that semester when it all came together there was obviously a feeling of accomplishment and celebration but more importantly, a bond happened of camaraderie between both of us, a brotherhood you might want to call it. After one of the last classes, we had probably the most significant walk that I've had as an adult. From the U of A education building to HUB mall, and what happened on this walk was both of us, maybe saddened a bit by the end of this project, but knowing this was really just a beginning, determined that this needed to continue, that Hiphop Kulture and education needed to move forward, and that we needed to figure out a way to come together on a regular basis and push this thing forward. But we're dealing with undefined things, y'know. It's like blind taste testing. You know you got somethin', you just don't know what it is, so you gotta taste it and figure it out.

Around this time, 2012, I had been flirting with an organization called the Temple of Hip Hop. A couple years earlier, on Facebook, I decided I would start a Temple of Hip Hop Canada page and then just walked away from it because life had taken me in other directions. Later, I was reading a book called *The Gospel of Hip Hop*, written by KRS-One, who is also a performer with Boogie Down Productions, and he had basically taken the path of Hip Hop and turned it into a spiritual teaching, and it was from this starting point that we decided to start a book club. To come together each week to discover what was in these pages, what this book was saying. What was happening by doing that was we were creating a Hiphop academic community.

Michael

And what was important for me about that transition is we went from a classroom environment where I was the teacher, to the basement of that bookstore where you were the teacher. That was a big deal for me.

Andre

Well that was a big deal for me, because you taught me how to run that class by going to your class. If I didn't go to your class I wouldn't have been able to pull that circle off. I mean it when I say I learnt a tremendous amount in that semester, I did. It was about how to engage students in discussion about stuff I don't know, and that's what was important to see you as a professor Michael, is that you didn't necessarily… like you knew what you were talking about, but there was so much you admitted that you don't know. Like, "I don't know where we're going with this but we're going to find out on the way," and this kind of walking with confidence with a blindfold was amazing to me.

Because it reminded me of what I was doing in my own early times, and that was only, that was a short period of not knowing before I taught myself, and I was a confident MC and Hip Hop practitioner, but when I saw you there it was like, "Holy," it was *that* space. That space worked so much, so much possibility, it really reignited something for me and allowed me to go in that circle and try and facilitate with confidence because I mean, when you got a couple PhD's sittin' there grillin' you about stuff and, y'know it's intimidating, y'know that. But I became comfortable with the content and we just started to go places and explore, and I mean, I just started to learn from you and hopefully you learned something too during those early times of Cipher5.

What was important to us in Cipher5, number one, was getting some clear definition on what Hiphop Kulture was so that we could move forward and explore, getting some ideas together and really just going into depth in what KRS-ONE was talking about. It's a fascinating book that inspires a lot of very intense discussion. But we got to a point of resolution with the book and this was probably the most important transition for Cipher5, in my opinion, because we came to a point where we had run this cycle, we had run through the book, we've had those big discussions and we needed to figure out where to go next and what was the next step for Cipher5. And I think we came to a conclusion that we had to be a working circle. We had to go back to the basement; I use my basement as a model for the next phase of Cipher5. We now get together, discuss issues in Hip Hop like whiteness and blackness, or global industries and local talent, postcolonialism, and we listen to hip-hop, watch documentaries, and make Hip Hop. When I say make Hip Hop: write songs, listen to songs, write graffiti, have DJs in the room, invite b-boys and b-girls. Have all elements represented and together on a regular basis to create a normality of our culture.

CONCLUSIONS

The goal for AST is to explain the production of group subjectivities through the making, sharing and using of aesthetic resources, as well as explain the role social and environmental processes play in *mediation* (Grossberg, 2010, 191), or in the production of individual subjectivities. AST has the potential to contribute to popular music studies and cultural studies by contextualizing the existing documentation of subcultures, communities of practice, fan culture etc., as examples of the use of aesthetic resources in the formation of group subjectivities. These many examples do not in themselves explain the formation of collective subjectivities, nor the formation of individual subjectivity (mediation). Further, global changes in production processes raise questions about their impacts on the production of collective and individual subjectivities. Guattari argues that it is necessary to understand, for instance, how the introduction of global capitalism, what he calls "Integrated World Capitalism" (IWC) (2008, 53), transforms the production of collective subjectivities located in consumption practices. There are a number of implications and further research questions for a cultural studies of music, and for the music education theory and practice that flow from this perspective. AST can shed light on the role music media plays in teaching and learning musical aesthetics, and how music fans and musicians are produced collectively. This approach helps to contribute a theoretical explanation for creativity, not as the product of a genius, but as the functioning of mediation. In this sense, mediation/creativity is no different from living or becoming an individual. And in this sense it is possible to consider Freire's conscientização as an informed mediation, and therefore education as the preparation for intelligent self-production, or self-design. I am currently exploring creativity/mediation/self-design as a critical pedagogy of music, where community creativity, liberation and critical thought can be understood as expressions of each other.

But there are also contradictions within Guattari's work that AST will help address. Guattari suggests that the formation of liberated group subjectivities requires a micro-political movement against mass production of IWC. But then he also says that the formation of subjectivities occurs through aesthetic resources that are simultaneously products of IWC. So is the production of group subjectivities, outside of IWC, currently possible? Guattari holds out hope that the localization of the production of subjectivities, a process he calls "molecular revolutions" (2008: 61), is possible, however it is unclear how this can occur in any societies that do not exclusively rely on the local production of their aesthetic resources. Further, it is unclear whether Guattari's concerns for the production of liberated subjectivities emerge from his analysis or are ideological. For example, does the mass production of aesthetic resources and the subsequent global collective subjectivities that follow necessarily have harmful consequences? If so, then there is no way Hip Hop and hiphoppas could be examples of liberated group subjectivities. An evaluation process is needed in order to determine whether people who identify with mass-produced aesthetic resources can simultaneously generate and exhibit liberated group subjectivities. I have suggested a dialogical process borrowed from Paulo Freire that led to the production of the transcript included in this chapter.

Andre describes a complex environment from which he developed a notion of creativity and selfhood that includes the built environment of the city, the social environment of his community, the economic environment of his family and the technological environment. He also describes affective territories that are more difficult to discuss theoretically, but are easy to recognize when reading his story. It is easy to feel the excitement, frustration, hope and fear in his story. These affective, emotional and sensual territories contribute to the mediation process and need to be included and accounted for. The production of the individual hiphoppa subjectivity seems to be liberatory even though Hip Hop is a mass-produced collective subjectivity widely distributed by IWC. Through Andre's story, it is possible to begin to identify the forces that contribute to the formation of "hiphoppa," and the creativity he exerts to distinguish his formulation of hiphoppa within the global collective subjectivity of Hip Hop.

Unlike the Keil-Feld discussions where knowledge production was an end in itself, Cipher5 has a context and a consequence that emerged from Hip Hop Kulture. In *The Gospel of Hip Hop,* the production of Hip Hop collective subjectivities is articulated in the oft-repeated phrase: I am Hip Hop. As Andre attested in our discussion, the practice of Hip Hop elements produces both Hip Hop (the culture/kulture) and Hiphoppas (the people who practice it). There is no distinction between making Hip Hop and being Hip Hop. That Hip Hop is a distinct aesthetic system that produces hiphoppas is captured in the semiotic play between "culture" and "kulture." KRS-ONE wrote that "true hiphoppas spell the full name of our culture with a k to signify our cultural uniqueness and our right to define ourselves ... Even beyond the right to define ourselves, Hip Hop Kulture is ... Hiphop reality" (2009: 108). His statement connects directly with Grossberg's description of mediation as the self-production of reality (2010, 191) and Guattari's (2008) discussion of the molecular revolution of creative group subjectivities. If music making, sharing and using produces cultural music works while simultaneously producing members of the culture, then it is fair to ask what kinds of subjectivities university music courses and culture are producing.

AST provides a starting point for an analysis of the production of subjectivity within formal music education. I have created the Aesthetic Systems Lab at MacEwan University to study the relationship between music production and the production of subjectivity, and its impact on music communities, cultures and music education. From the work that has led to the development of AST and the culture circle method, I have come to see a need for cross-cultural methods of aesthetic analysis in the hopes of identifying bridges or pathways to new forms of university music education. For instance, a current project at the lab is a study of Hip Hop music theory and aesthetic judgment. The study pairs a group of university-trained composers together with a collection of Hip Hop producers to share and compare methods of compositional practice. We are investigating the processes of learning, how they occur, the role of technology and how one knows and learns what is "good" and "bad" within a given cultural system. The goal of the study is to theorize the relationship between collective aesthetic subjectivities, individual subjectivities and creativity. We hope that these outcomes will result in better insights into other ways of evaluating musical skills so that we might alter entrance requirements to better support and reflect the diverse musicians in our community. The hiphoppas I work with in Edmonton possess significant musical capacities, but the MacEwan music department does not have entrance requirements and curriculum developed in a way that recognizes such musicians. It is my hope, and the hope of students working in my lab, that a better understanding of different ways of conceptualizing the production of musical subjectivities may lead to expanding what the department recognizes as capable musicians. Moreover, it is my hope that as a faculty, we might come to understand our role in the production of new collective subjectivities as a method of contributing new and perhaps healthier ways of being together and being ourselves.

NOTES

[1] Originally published as "Aesthetic Systems Theory: Doing Hiphop Aesthetics Research Together". *MusiCultures. Journal of the Canadian Society for Traditional Music*, Community-engaged research special edition, 2015, pp. 34–53. Reprinted with permission.

[2] I would like to thank the members of Cipher5 for their contribution to this article. There have been too many discussions with too many people to name everyone but special thanks goes to Chris Cousino (aka DJ Dice) and Don Welsh (ID) who have contributed a great deal of support for this research. Big thanks to Diana Pearson who read every version of this paper and provided substantial feedback along the way. Thanks to Andre Hamilton for all of the sharing and growing over the last few years. Finally, thanks to MacEwan University Research Office, especially Meghan Abbott, and the research support I have received from the MacEwan University Faculty of Fine Arts and Communications.

[3] Spelling *culture* as *kulture* makes a distinction between the general category of contemporary culture as the field of mass cultural production (culture industry) and Hiphop Kulture as an autonomous ethico-aesthetic movement to regain the anthropological understanding of culture as the lifeways of a community.

[4] Emcee is the MC or master of ceremonies most often associated with rapping. B-boy and b-Girls are break-boys/girls, sometimes called breakdancers. DJs, or disk jockeys, improvise with records.

[5] Angela Impey noted the value of *Participatory Action Research* for ethnomusicology: "Through the application of participatory research methodologies, the process of documentation could begin to stimulate dialogue and exchange between Khula residents, and could provide a platform for people to address issues of identity, meaning and community building. The development of a narrative for eco- and cultural tourist consumption would therefore be linked with an initiative that sought to actively recover the communities' histories, identities and traditional knowledge systems, and operate as a process upon which other kinds of community interventions could be explored." (2002, 13; see also Carr & Kemmis, 1986; Fine & Torre, 2008; Noffke & Somekh, 2009).

AESTHETIC GOVERNMENTALITY & SUBJECTIVATION IN AESTHETICS SYSTEMS

I always know something, really know it, when I take it apart and put it back together. Taking a machine apart is always satisfying but if you ever want it to work again you learn the importance of carefully sketching the location of every screw and wire. For me it was a toaster. I not only learned mechanical and electrical things about how the toast popped and how electricity was transformed into heat, I also learned about globalization. I was stunned to discover that a toaster does not come into the world fully formed, that it is a collection of component parts manufactured in factories all over the world and only later assembled into my toaster. It also occurred to me that people, each with a family and a set of needs that may or may not be met were all part of that toaster. I have never again looked at a toaster in the same light. Tearing apart the family toaster also taught me about the complexities of active learning, systems and political economy. When you are engaged in discovery there is always a chance to be stunned by powerful and transformative insights that could never have been planned and have more value than being told. I could have been told about all of the things that I learned, and perhaps I was, but I remember the toaster and the excitement of discovering. Foucauldian Discourse Analysis (Arribas-Ayllon, 2008; Kendall, 1999) is like this. It is a practice of taking social, not mechanical, things apart and trying to put them back together. And not only is the practice the same, but so too are the benefits and potential rewards.

Foucault taught us to start by paying attention to what is said. These statements form complex networks—the machines of social life—that he calls discourse. Taking the discourse apart is called critique, it is the act of breaking up what we think we know into parts. This is also called deconstruction and is quite popular as a method of critique. What distinguishes Foucauldian Discourse Analysis is putting the parts back together and discovering how the components are productive, that is, what the parts produce when they are connected in a system. In this essay I will apply Foucauldian Discourse Analysis to Popular Music Pedagogy in an effort to do two things, to understand the objectives of popular music education, and to propose a research-based undergraduate pedagogy for popular music studies.

POLITICS OF POPULAR MUSIC PEDAGOGY: EDUCATION FOR EMANCIPATION OR LIBERATION

After completing my PhD on the social and economic impact of festivals in western Canada I turned my attention to the questions of cultural transmission. It began with the musing of a long time music festival organizer who joked that even if her organization went bankrupt, and the press did not notice, thousands of volunteers would show up and build the festival, the audience would arrive and take their places, the vendors would arrive and set up and begin selling their wares, the audio company would arrive and set up their gear, local presenters would line up artists and the event would begin. Amusing as it was we were only partly joking. There is a force that we deal with in cultural research. It is unnerving, mysterious and very complex. We do ourselves an injustice by reducing the mystery to a little word: culture. But we cannot turn back the clock now, we are stuck always starting our explanations by trying to show that culture is not a noun but a territory or assemblage of productive forces, like a Rhizome (Deleuze & Guatarri, 1983, 1987), or maybe The Blob. Culture is how and what people do as Gavin Kendall and Gary Wickham (1999) noted of Michel Foucault, for him culture is not about meaning, it is about administration.

Teaching and learning play an important role in culture. So upon completing my festival research I began a postdoc at the University of Alberta Centre for Teaching and Learning and it was there that I first read Professor Green's (2008) Music, Informal Learning and the School: A New Classroom Pedagogy. I turned my attention to urban aesthetic informal learning and after a series of twists and turns I started working with leading members of the local Hip Hop community. Our partnership has led to the creation of Cipher5, a community-based Hiphop Kulture research environment that has provided an opportunity to study Hiphop informal learning the creation and use of local microhistories, to develop cultural studies methods for the study of aesthetic education, and more recently how action research might contribute to the philosophy of aesthetics and aesthetics education. During the completion of the most recent phase, that for the first time included undergraduate research assistants, another possibility emerged, that Cipher5 might provide an alternative undergraduate learning environment. The value of undergraduate research and its contribution to learning has been shown (Brew, 1995; Williston, 2007), my aim in this article is to show the connection between critical aesthetics research, teaching and learning of popular music history, and the development of critical thinking.

The search has to begin with identifying the pedagogical objectives of popular music pedagogical practices. In 1999, Göran Folkestad, an invited guest editor for a special edition of the International Journal of Music Education, reflects on this task:

> During the last decades, a vast body of research has investigated popular music as a musical phenomenon, describing the musical content and function of especially Pop and Rock music...In the present issue, the emphasis is on popular music as an educational phenomenon. Accordingly, as popular forms of music in music education is the main aim and specific subject field of the publication, and the intend main target group is music teachers all over the world, the articles in this issue have a focus on, and include descriptions and

studies of important aspects of formal as well as informal musical teaching/ learning situations, which hopefully will be of value to music education internationally. Hence, one of the intentions of this special focus issue is to encourage the IJME readership to explore new directions, and to document interesting ways in which music educators can incorporate popular music into their day-to-day teaching. (2000: 1)

In the same issue, David G. Hebert and Patricia Shehan Campbell contribute "Rock Music in American Schools: Positions and Practices Since the 1960s" and position the study of popular music pedagogy relative to rock's counter-establishment narrative: "These pioneering essays [in the 1960s] advocated the use of popular and rock music in classrooms, even as FBI director J. Edgar Hoover continued to carry the larger societal view, that such music 'is repulsive to right-thinking people and can have serious effects in our young people" (14). Hebert and Campbell document the gradual incorporation of popular music into the music education classroom but the authors provide little indication that the incorporation impacted pedagogical approaches. There is no evidence in fact that music educators are drawing from Popular Music Studies research or the developing cultural studies of the period, or the critical pedagogy developed from the application of critical theory (Adorno, 1991; Benjamin, 1968, 1977) to schooling (Freire, 2001; hooks, 1994, 2003, 2010; Ibrahim, 2014; Kincheloe, 2005, 2010; Steinberg, 2001). Popular Music education seems to be the application popular music repertoire in an existing classroom-based music education practice:

> Lessons in rock music may require young students to engage with a broader diversity of musical skills, concepts, and technologies than they otherwise might. Students who study the music will no doubt broaden their understanding of music as a phenomenon of expression of our time. They may be drawn through such studies to recognize the relevance of their technical skills in relation to both amateur and professional performing opportunities outside the classroom. The participation by students in popular music through formal educational opportunities in school can be an invaluable means by which they may develop improvisation, composition and arranging skills – all of which are fundamental components of musicianship throughout the world. (14)

This approach to using the content of the popular music industry as the organizing logic of the study of popular music seems consistent in popular music history as well. As a quick survey of popular music textbooks illustrates, most are organized on a "coverage model" of popular music history. The coverage model is an approach historical survey where, as is suggested in the name, as much important historical data as possible is surveyed. There are perhaps two issues here. First, most of us would agree that importance in these texts is determined by economic success. But we do not seem to have developed theories of cultural valuation that help us critique these successes and therefore find ourselves at odds with what we know from the study of the artworlds (Becker, 1984). The second issue with the coverage model is its facts first approach that has been called "wrong-headed" and "a failure on its own terms" by cognitive psychologists and history educators (Sipress & Voelker, 2011: 1051). Many music history survey classes, including my own sometimes and unfortunately, "emphasizes the transmission of knowledge from instructor to student, typically focusing on surface detail in order to get through the material" using a method that is "deeply embedded within the culture of our profession" with objectives that are "rarely discussed" (Crain, 2014: 302). Interestingly, objections to the coverage model are not new. In an 1898 American Historical Association criticism was framed this way: "the chief purpose [of historical education] is not to fill the boy's head with a mass of material which he may perchance put forth again when a college examiner demands its production" (cited in, Sipress & Voelker, 2011: 1052).

Since a critique of the application of the coverage model to music history joins an already century long discussion Foucault's observation that "models of classroom practice have not changed much over an extended period of time" (Thomas, 2008: 151) is relevant. It is perhaps necessary to ask why these models are so long-lasting. Perhaps the resistance to change can be found in the way the coverage model is thought to satisfy core-learning objectives. What are the objectives of our pedagogies? Are we interested in creating freethinking and critical students? I think most of us would agree. Perhaps the difference comes down to how we get our students to this point and perhaps this comes down to how we believe educational transformation occurs. Immanuel Kant's explanation of enlightenment seem to capture the heart of this intervention:

> Enlightenment is man's emergence from his self-imposed nonage. Nonage is the inability to use one's own understanding without another's guidance. This nonage is self-imposed if its cause lies not in lack of understanding but in indecision and lack of courage to use one's own mind without another's guidance. Dare to know! (Sapere aude.) "Have the courage to use your own understanding," is therefore the motto of the enlightenment.

Educational intervention is meant as a technique to free thinking subjects. And perhaps it is the study of these techniques of intervention, the scholarship of teaching and learning, that require our attention. Foucault explains Kant's text this way:

> Kant indicates right away that the "way out" that characterizes Enlightenment is a process that releases us from the status of "immaturity." And by "immaturity," he means a certain state of our will that makes us accept someone else's authority to lead us in areas where the use of reason is called for. Kant gives three examples: we are in a state of "immaturity" when a book takes the place of our understanding, when a spiritual director takes the place of our conscience, when a doctor decides for us what our diet is to be. (Let us note in passing that the register of these three critiques is easy to recognize, even though the text does not make it explicit.) In any case, Enlightenment is

defined by a modification of the preexisting relation linking will, authority, and the use of reason. (Foucault, 1984: 33)

At this point we can raise the critique that the "contemporary critical tradition continues a nineteenth century view of social redemption through schooling" (Popkewitz & Brennan, 1998, 7). So where does the coverage model come from and why is it so difficult to change if all along we have been following Kant's suggestion that education is the development of independent and therefore critical thought. Perhaps one explanation for this lies in Foucault's explanation for the development of techniques of discipline in schooling.

In Discipline and Punish (1995) Foucault illustrated that the 19th century view of social redemption (liberation) and discipline were in line with each other. It was thought impractical to allow individuals to figure themselves out for themselves, knowledge and society had become too complex. Just as the complexity of the developing 19th century factory required new practices of discipline in order to produce goods so too did productive elementary education require "details of surveillance specified and integrated into the teaching relationship" (175):

> We have here a sketch of an institution of the 'mutual' type in which three procedures are integrated into a single mechanism: teaching proper, the acquisition of knowledge by the very practice of the pedagogical activity and a reciprocal, hierarchized observation. A relation of surveillance, defined and regulated, is inscribed at the heart of the practice of teaching, not as an additional or adjacent part, but as mechanism that is inherent to it and which increases its efficiency. (Foucault, 1995: 176)

So we have inherited two approaches to productive education. On the one hand there is the Kantian model of education as intellectual emancipation and on the other there is the model of liberatory education. The conflict comes down to a question of whether the objectives of education are emancipation of the individuals by themselves, as critical pedagogues would have it, or is it the cultivation of methods of students' self-surveillance that leads to a students liberation expressed in the performance of 'correct thinking'. It seems that the coverage model is an example of the liberatory model of education that may have come up short on its contribution to educational liberation. But I am not going to argue this point further because I think it is a matter of pedagogical choice and further study. I have chosen emancipatory education because I feel more comfortable using critical pedagogical approaches. Perhaps this is in keeping with my personal history of aesthetic education.

THE FIRST RULE OF AESTHETIC FIGHT CLUB

I feel it is important to situate the study of music history through the student's study of the present, not only because this is Foucault's method but also for more personal reasons. My engagement with music education and its pedagogy did not emerge strictly from an interest in developing better popular music history pedagogy. In fact, I never set out to be a professor, nor a popular music history teacher. Before I came to this I was a musician and fight club aesthetic philosopher. It all started innocently enough. I was born into a musical family in an eastern Canadian small town. I wanted to play music so my parents sent me to classical piano lessons. For many young people this is very normal but for me, growing up in a traditional music community surrounded by musicians who played regularly and around the house, it was out of the ordinary to go to a stranger's home to play a massive piano adorned with gilded frames and busts of important looking fellows. While my older relatives played what I would learn to call folk and country music I was learning classical music. I was learning to read and write music. Reading and writing was real learning. After a few months of lessons I wanted to play with someone. A fiddler began playing a tune and I locked up. I sat at the piano staring at the keys, the emptiness of the music stand, and I felt defeated. I had no idea what to do. I could not play. I could read, but not play. I became frustrated with my learning, a frustration that would continue for many years and would plant a seed.

Finally, I came into possession of an electric bass and a small amplifier. Soon after I was asked to join a band. The logic was that I had been taking piano lessons for many years and that I could read and write music. Clearly I knew what I was doing. I was unsure if this logic held up, since I had never had lessons on bass, but I wanted to be in a band so I kept my reservations to myself. I showed up to the house and lugged my gear into the basement. The guitarist, a really skinny kid with a crazy tuft of red hair and big glasses announced that he had written a few songs. He switched on his amp, and I followed. The drummer sat down at a rickety stool, his drums tilting quite unnaturally. The electricity hummed. The click of pickups, a sound I will always love. And then, in a blur, we rocked.

We made a racket for years and even toured a little. We recorded tapes regularly sometimes narrowly missing getting signed, more than once, to one little indie label or another. In the mid-90s there was a feverish rush that accompanied SubPop's interest in Canadian rock bands. That thing they called Grunge was huge, though we cared little. We knew it was really something altogether beyond a few Seattle bands. It was a movement.

We were a bunch of noisy, punky kids who drew equally from Sam Cooke, Sonic Youth, the Ramones, the Pogues, and perhaps most importantly, each other. We were lots of bands you have never heard and will never hear of. We made music for lots of reasons too. Sometimes for the fun of it, the entertainment of it, because we thought we were cool, sometimes probably for the girls (although I don't actually remember this being the case). But ultimately it was politically charged independent cultural production. We knew a little about Punk music, enough to know DIY, and perhaps some among us would identify with one of those lineages. I was certainly not aware of it. I did not even know I was in a punk band. This might sound strange to you but I had no pretense of being in a punk band. I thought punk bands were cool and my band was just weird. We just made music that kind of sounded a bit like a few things, but mostly we worked hard to sound like us. Eventually we would just call it grunge of course, but for us it was much more than that. It was culture jamming.

Everywhere we looked large companies were telling us what to eat, what to wear, what to buy and what to like. Advertisement was the technology of persuasion, the TV, radio, and magazines were its carriers. The media celebrated the successes of the marketplace, but we did not celebrate. We were in a battle for mind-share, and we were losing. But we learned about Guerilla techniques, about culture jamming, and were taking part in late night battles for intellectual freedom. We were engaged in cultural critique. Sometimes it was about posting red stickers blazoned with large white words like 'Watching TV' directly under the STOP on stop signs. One Monday morning commuters were met with a stream of challenges at every stop sign in our inner-city core, STOP—Watching TV, STOP—Believing the Media, STOP—Buying Happiness. Our little Guerilla tactics moved seamlessly between art and political action. For us there was no distinction, there was only political action. Either you were aware of the struggle or you were already lost to the machine. For those that were aware of the struggle, the enemy was the machine of industry, and for us the first rule was independence. When I first saw Fight Club I felt the movie captured our ethics. The first rule of Aesthetic Fight Club: make culture your own.

AESTHETIC GOVERNMENTALITY AND AESTHETIC SUBJECTIVATION

The coverage model has helped shed light on genre but has obscured the horizon of aesthetic power and the politics of its practice and the implication of this for youth. The consequences of this oversight are far reaching as the emergence of Critical Youth Studies has tried to show (Ibrahim & Steinberg, 2014). If we fail to see that youth have been using aesthetic practices to make culture since at least the 1950s and maybe even since the 1930s then we fail to even begin to understand our students' current lives and therefore, as teachers, fail to produce adequate theories of youth and fail to prepare youth for their own critical engagement and educational emancipation. I think there is plenty of evidence to show that youth know what is at stake. The choice to belong to an aesthetic system impacts the formation of social networks, wardrobe, recreational activities, interests, drug use or lack of use, practices of hygiene, attitudes towards sexuality, and much more. Choosing the music we love initiates us into systems of communication that marks us as members of aesthetic culture with all of the responsibilities and freedoms. And while we sense the importance of this choice, and know that there are consequences or at least implications to these choices, there is still too little preparation available for youth in schools. I do not think this is because teachers do not care, but because we have yet to develop a pedagogy that assists us in engaging in this field. My interest in the remainder of the essay is to forward a method of aesthetic research that may replace the coverage model by focusing learning on undergraduate students' present engagement with popular music aesthetics. The starting point is to take seriously the power of popular music culture and its role in trans-forming youth. For some cultural studies oriented readers this is familiar territory. The difference is methodological and pedagogical perhaps. I am not engaging with popular culture in an attempt to break its power, nor am I provided methods of correct thinking about the contents of culture instead I am forwarding a research method that teachers and students use together to document their own experiences. This critical pedagogy of popular music culture, developed on Foucault's model of Discourse Analysis, supports students to critique how genres are cultures built by practices of truth (knowledge-power), administration of bodies (governmentality), and practices of making yourself (techniques of subjectivation).

AESTHETIC BIOPOWER IN YOUTH PRACTICES OF SUBJECTIVATION

In youth-oriented education practice it seems necessary to theorize, along with students, the forces of aesthetic governmentality and techniques of subjectivation that form aesthetic cultures. To illustrate the tension between aesthetic governmentality and aesthetic subjectivation I will once again draw upon personal testimony, this time from, Professor Joe Kincheloe's childhood discovery of the blues and its transformative impact, his introduction into what he has calls blues epistemology (Kincheloe, 2008: 143–169):

> I had to learn to play this music. But where did a white boy go to learn the blues? I tried two dollar a week piano lessons, but when I told my teacher that I wanted to play rock and the blues, she laughed out loud. I don't think you want to learn that kind of trash she told me, as she directed me once again to play "Country Gardens" from my piano book. My heart sank. Where could you learn something viewed as something so based and worthless as rock and the "nigger music" it thought inappropriate? Luckily for me as I was asking these questions, I discovered a local African-American blues band playing many of the same songs I was listening to on WLAC. I was entranced by the Baddaddies and went by myself to see them wherever they played around Kingsport.

> I watch the keyboard player intently as he made the sounds, the blue notes that were so central to rock and blues piano. To my adolescent mind the sounds were secret mysteries—I had no idea how to produce them. Desperate to learn I realized I have but one choice: I would have to go and watch the Baddaddies practice. While in the contemporary era that might not sound like too difficult a feat, for 12 or 13-year-old hillbilly kid in a racially segregated place and time it was quite transgressive. Finding out where the band practiced, I walked a couple of miles one Saturday afternoon to the in racist language of Tennessee in the early 1960s 'nigger town'. I knocked on the door and finally one of the bands friends let me in. 'Can I watch the band practice?' I asked. Suspicious and surprised by the presence of a white kid in this circumstance, the young man nodded for me to come back to the practice room. I felt like I was in the

inner sanctum of some forbidden Temple. I spotted the piano player and sat on a box as close to him as possible.

Everyone looked at me with the same apprehensive gaze of the guy at the door. The room smells like stale cigarettes, beer, and pot. I watch for hours as the band added new songs to their playlist. No one spoke to me and I spoke to no one. I was simply thankful that my presence was tolerated. When the band decided to end the practice I thank each of the musicians for letting me watch and listen. For the next couple of Saturdays I followed the same ritual, trying to observe everything that the keyboardist did during the songs and it's relation to what the rest of the band was playing. At the end of the third practice, the piano player turned and looked me in the eyes for the first time since my curious appearance. Though no words had been spoken about the music or me, he had discerned that I was interested in playing the piano. 'You wanna play the blues piano?' he asked with a laugh—a snicker that said to me 'you seem kind of serious about this, white boy.' Realizing that this was the chance I had been hoping for, I stood up and mimicked his manner and look at me. 'Yes,' I said with all the gravitas filtered through a cool irreverence that I could project.

The next 10 minutes change my life. He showed me the basic 'theoretical' structure of the blues. Then he paraded a few blues piano 'licks' that involve sliding off one note to another and making discordant sounds by concurrently playing notes that were only one-halfstep apart. In a matter of moments the hidden structure of the blues and rock were revealed to me like the Apostle Paul on Highway 61. I mustered all my powers of concentration to remember every spoken word and every played note of the hollowed insights—the subjugated musical knowledge—granted to me... I ran all the way home, going over in my mind everything I had learned. I rushed to the door and sat down at my mother's antique piano and practiced the licks for hours.

The three licks formed the grounding for everything I have subsequently done on the piano in 42 years of playing rock and blues. More importantly, this experience of becoming a researcher of knowledges not necessarily respected at a particular historical moment by dominant culture helped shape my understanding of both epistemology and pedagogy. (Kincheloe, 2008, 17–18)

Kincheloe's testimony brings together technologies of production (learning to make the sounds), signification (the blues), domination (the subjugation of African American cultural practice), and self (his identification with a form of music that he was not supposed to connect with, his struggle to make that connection and the subsequent lifelong impact). While aesthetic cultures have dominating structures of control that attempt to shape the proper subjects to itself, what Foucault called governmentality (2004, 2010), there is always the potential for these structures to be transgressed or innovated upon. It is in this sense that biopower is not only domination but also the field of power of shaping the body in new ways, the subject becomes an object to itself (2004). Biopower exists in the administration of communication, in the contents of communication and the implications of its use. It is through communication that subjects are capable of thinking, find techniques and practices of self-formation, innovate, and produce networks of mutual becoming with other subjects. The process of self-formation occurs through the use of techniques of subjectivation made available in aesthetics cultures. I am afraid this approach to genre does not make the study of popular music easier, in fact it does quite the opposite, it complicates it quite a great deal, and necessarily.

CRITICAL PEDAGOGY OF POPULAR MUSIC THROUGH AESTHETIC SYSTEMS

This approach, I have called the cultural Aesthetic Systems is a critical pedagogical approach to genre built upon a variety of sources from aesthetics, critical theory, critical pedagogy and cultural studies. I have been influenced by Arnold Berleant's theories of aesthetic experience, aesthetic education and the aesthetic field (1991, 1992, 2000, 2004, 2010) itself informed by John Dewey (1916, 1938). My ideas have been further influenced by Jacques Ranciere's political aesthetics (2000, 2005, 2007, 2010) and aesthetic community (De Boever, 2011; Ranciere, 1991; Robson, 2005) and by Nichlas Bourriaud's relational aesthetics (2002) all politicized through powerful critiques of western modernity and aesthetics provided by bell hooks (1990, 1994, 2003, 2004, 2008, 2010, 2013), Walter Mignolo (2000, 2011) Garatri Spivak (2012), Linda Tuhiwai Smith (2012) a activated by critical pedagogy (Freire, 2001; Giroux, 2004, 2009; Kincheloe, 2010; Steinberg, 2001, 2009; Stinson, 1998) and Handel Wright's urging to take cultural studies personally (2003). At the core of this method is the idea that genre is the emergent property of an aesthetic system, understood as a discourse constructed in the exchange of statements. For Foucault, discourse emerges from networks of statements. As music scholars I think this provides us an excellent starting point. Aesthetic discourse is a system of textual, oral, aural, visual, and gestural (perhaps olfactory?) "statements" that get organized and used in such a way as to produce aesthetic systems that need to be understood *beyond* genres.

I propose a Foucauldian Discourse Analysis for aesthetics build on the initial study four modes: (a) textual, (b) aural, (c) visual and, (d) gestural. These four modes can be further grouped into two groups: the textual-aural and the visual-gestural. My contention is that genres emerge through aesthetic statements that make sense within a group of statements. All of the content of a genre, from fan statements, music, videos, performer interviews, magazines and fan lifestyles, attitudes and habits can be understood as contributing to a discourse through the use of these four modes. Further, by comparing Aesthetic Statements within a discourse at any particular historical time students can begin to identify aesthetic governmentality and subjectivation as strategies that they may be personally experiencing. I do not have space in this article to provide examples of the application of this approach beyond an invitation to use the modes I will discuss below for the analysis of the personal statements above. I would encourage readers to return to these narratives and to apply the Aesthetic Discourse Analysis strategy discussed below because I feel that much of the value of this article becomes clearer in the practice of the technique.

Textual-Aural

Every mode has its affordance and its counter affordance. The textual mode progresses linearly letter-by-letter, word-by-word, phrase-by-phrase constantly adding ideas and moving (in English) left to right. From the perspective of Foucault's four technologies, the production of the text, writing invites the writer and reader into a system of social signification that is often rigidly fixed by cultural conventions. The written word is a dominating medium that is often the last word in a dispute, and hence the power of written contracts and conventions. Finally, as Foucault pointed out in great length in his final work on Writing as a Technology of Self, text has historically played an important role helping to shape and order the structure of the self.

Foucault's essay analyses a passage from Athanasius's Vita Antoni about writing the self that involve 'the actions and movements of our souls as though to make them mutually known to one another, and let us be sure that out of shame at being known, we will cease sinning and have nothing perverse in our hearts' (cited in Foucault, 1997b, p. 234). 'Self-writing' ... 'offsets the dangers of solitude' and exposes our deeds to a possible gaze; at the same time the practice works on thoughts as well as actions, which brings it into line with the role of confession (in the early Christian literature). It permits, at the same time, a retrospective analysis of 'the role of writing in the philosophical culture of the self just prior to Christianity: its close tie with apprenticeship; its applicability to movements of thought; its role as a test of truth' (Foucault, 1997b, p. 235). Reading and writing are part of 'arts of the self 'which contribute to what Foucault calls the 'aesthetics of existence' and also a basis for the government of self and others.

But for all that writing affords we all know that writing has pretty obvious counter affordances that we exploit regularly. For instance, I can write 'Good Morning' and I can then say this in quite a variety of ways, as anyone who has done any stage of screen acting knows only too well. The oral mode, that mode of speech, and the aural mode, the mode of listening, emerge in the counter affordance of literacy. Literacy, for all of the claims to its permanence, has no fixed subject. No one belongs to the written word, its author floats until it is spoken and only then does the text become concrete in the world. When the text is spoken, or in our case, sung or rapped, the words are owned by a subject, and they tend to seem to emerge from a creative self. We know only too well how difficult it is to analyze a musical performance and separate the textual mode from the aural mode. When words are made audible they tend to get locked to the voice, and from the voice to the body, and from the body to the imagination of the speaker. The sound of the words, not the text any longer, but the sound signifiers become the center of our interest. The affordance of the aural mode (listening) is geolocation, when we hear we do not hear in the general, but the specific and only the specific. Just as it is impossible for a text to exist only in one moment and in one place so too is it impossible for a sound to be general, it always exists in only one place and only one time.

But this geolocating has undergone significant changes due to the industrial revolution of sound technology. The aural mode, which would always be geolocated in your physical presence was able to be separated from the physical body of its source. This separation, a practice Canadian composer and sound theorist R. Murray Schafer named schizophonia, created a horizon for signification. Once unhinged from direct signification the aural mode entered into a game of signification that characterizes our present situation and provided the context for the emersion of aesthetic culture organized around music.

Visual-Gestural

Very quickly, perhaps immediately, the aural mode was signified by the visual mode. Even older than the textual mode, the visual mode reaches back to ancient practices of signification. It might seem odd for the uninitiated to think of the visual mode as being the most ancient practice of signification until you begin to draw a confusing but continuous line between Facebook photos and Alexandrian coins. We signify ourselves in much the same way as we always have in western society, by our face, our clothes, our particular practices of grooming. Our facial and bodily features, the choices we make in the decoration and adornment of our bodies are all practices of signification that not only can be read but are composed and read moment to moment. The visual mode includes colors, textures, shapes and lines it is everything that we see. It is the settings that carry so much meaning and frame expectations for the social acts that will unfold. And it is in the unfolding of these acts where the gestural mode emerges.

The gestural mode is as old as the visual but has taken on a much greater importance with the invention of moving pictures. The gestural mode will include the changing of the shape of the mouth, which when signified we understand as a smile or the changing position of the legs, when signified suggests walking, running, dancing, standing and also more complex ideas like excitement, boredom or even still more complex ideas such as masculinity, femininity, sexuality, religiosity et cetera. The visual can be a context for the central action of the gestural, but one should not rush to construct hierarchies. It is the practices of signification across four modes at once that we are interested in, and through learning to identify the modes, by separating them out for the purposes of content analysis we may get beyond genre to the practices of production, signification, hierarchy and self that form the aesthetic system.

CONCLUSION

While it is well known that Foucault is interested in power, what is often missed, or at least under emphasized, is that power is not a special force that can be discovered, it is the productive effects of discourse upon the body. Discourse is a product of four techniques or technologies that can be used as a method of research into popular music cultures by identifying the ways that aesthetic statements, built using modes, produce an aesthetic system that gives shape to history and shapes the communication and bodies of subjects. An aesthetic system emerges from the use of four techniques:

1. The techniques of production
2. The technique of signification
3. The technique of domination
4. The technique of self

These techniques/technologies are strategies utilized for the production of aesthetic statements, built by using resources (modes) available from what Foucault calls the archive, for the production of culture—the administration of bodies and things. Put most simply we communicate using the communication resources that we have learned. We do not independently create a language, we inherit it (from the archive), we learn its structures through practice and experimentation, and this practice governs not only our statements but also how we use them. But we also innovate and improvise with these same resources. We say things that no one else has said and in the process of doing this, of learning and of improvising, we provide a shape for ourselves we call identity. We make ourselves a subject to our self. We use aesthetic systems like we use language. There is a great deal more going on in our aesthetic education than just inheriting a history of song names and performers; we also inherit social structures and ultimately the beginnings of ourselves. While I'm not sure this method of aesthetic self-critique will necessarily lead to intellectual emancipation, I do think it provides an alternative approach to the coverage model and one that puts the lives of music students, their aesthetic practices, their learned and improvised practices of communication, and their interest in themselves and others at the center of their educational development. And this seems like a good use of class time.

CRITICAL PEDAGOGY OF AESTHETICS EDUCATION[1]

Instead of choosing between instilling youth with an appreciation of artistic culture (art history) or training youth for professional life in art production (performance), youth art educators might choose *conscientização* through critical aesthetic education. Paulo Freire's *conscientização* "can be literally translated as the process used to raise somebody's awareness" (Cruz, 2013, p. 171) but is richer than this. It is "the process in which men [and women], not as recipients, but as knowing subjects, achieve a deepening awareness both of the sociocultural reality that shapes their lives and of their capacity to transform that reality" (Freire, 1970, p. 519).

From Plato, to Matthew Arnold, to Theador Adorno, it has been understood that youth are molded by cultural education. Plato encouraged art education that would influence the development of youth taste in ways that would support the state. Arnold worried about the loss of culture with the rise of cultural industries. Adorno, relatedly, worried about cultural industries transforming people into empty-headed consumers powerless to tell good art from bad. Thinkers in this school all champion aesthetic education by way of cultural appreciation. It is thought that youth taught to appreciate the masterworks of European culture will come into possession of *culture*. I am going to suggest a different approach: that youth are already fully engaged in culture, and that in a democracy, we do not need to instill culture from positions of power, but instead to provide teachers and youth opportunities and capacities to make decisions about their participation in the formation of their culture. Instead of making aesthetic decisions for youth, we might develop an approach to art education that is a 'critical' study of aesthetic. I believe this will lead to what we really want, *conscientização*, and there is good reason for this hunch.

Since at least the 1950s, but perhaps since the jazz age of the 1930s, progressive youth art cultures have been engines of individual and social transformation. At the center of these transformations (think jazz, counter-culture, festival culture, DIY, Punk, Riot Grrrl, Hiphop Kulture, EDM) are processes of consciousness-raising related to art production, aesthetic *conscientização*. To understand how this occurs, we need to develop *cultural studies of aesthetics*.

But why do this? What is wrong with the current form of aesthetic education? First, there is little in the way of aesthetic education actually being offered. Nearly all art education is either art production (doing it) or art history (what has been done), and little time is placed on the hows and whys of art practice. Practices that are little studied are seldom taught. This means, in the North American context, that youth are surrounded by generations of popular music forms, many of them historically significant, that are still not taught in school. There is no point waiting for school curriculum and school text books to catch up. Instead, I propose teaching students to do cultural studies of aesthetics, to transform art appreciation classes into cultural studies of aesthetics classes.

AESTHETICS

bell hooks (1990) told us that "many underclass black people who do not know conventional academic theoretical language are thinking critically about aesthetics. The richness of their thoughts is rarely documented in books" (p. 112). I want to expand on this and say that many *people* are thinking critically about aesthetics, but do not have access to Aesthetics, an elite philosophical practice of writing about art. But aesthetics does not need to be something only philosophers are permitted to do. Quite the contrary: philosophical aesthetics is not the only discourse on aesthetics.

In fact, an exhaustive study of all academic aesthetics may still not prepare you to understand the Hiphop Kulture concept of *flow*, or the jazz concept of *swing*. If you wish to study fine-arts culture, then you may delight in reading philosophical aesthetics. But if you delight in the deep throb of an electronic kick drum, those books may not be the place for you. Much popular music culture is not related to European notions of creativity or expressiveness. These cultural forms developed in North American urban contexts and are distinct. So, if, as Plato and Adorno noted, aesthetic education informs consciousness, what is at stake by not recognizing that popular culture is aesthetically distinct from Fine-Art Culture? To answer this question, we need to have a definition of aesthetics.

In his question about understanding reason's role in the Enlightenment, 18th century philosopher, Alexander Baumgarten, began to puzzle over a complex relationship between intellect and perception. Baumgarten noted that the senses work to acquire information from the environment, fed to the brain by way of perception. The senses provide complex information that the mind works to sort out. The mind sorts sense information into meaning.

Baumgarten recognized that art meaning emerged from the crossroads of conceptual, emotional, historical, and physical information. He and others recognized this as a new and interesting subject area that he called Aesthetics, the science of how things are cognized by means of the senses. Unfortunately, this tidy definition would not last long. By 1790, Immanuel Kant redefined aesthetics as the study of the beautiful, a definition that has exerted far greater impact and limited 'what' the subjects practitioners might be equipped to survey. Perhaps if aesthetics had remained a scientific study of the relationship between perception and meaning in relation to art, it may have become a cross-cultural study of expressive practices, contributing a proto-anthropology of art. But this was not to be so.

A CULTURAL DEFINITION OF AESTHETICS

In recent years, there have been some signs of a return to Baumgarten's ideas. German complexity sociologist, Niklas Luhmann (2000), has suggested a redefinition of aesthetics: the study of perception and communication in relation to art. Luhmann began with the premise that the inner world of each human is separated from other inner worlds. Within each inner world, a constant flood of information is registered by the nervous system. This data is registered by the brain and understood by the mind. The mind, what Luhmann called the psychic system, deals with information by treating it as communication resources. For Luhmann, human experience is made possible by communication. We understand the world by first internalizing a communication system; only then can we 'understand' the world. Learning, therefore, the acquisition of communication resources, opens up ways of knowing the world. Further, he argued that social groups are formed by and through communication. From here it can be said that aesthetics is the study of art as a *special form of communication* that plays with familiar or unfamiliar communication resources in familiar or unfamiliar ways; that meddles with the links that bind perception to meaning.

Separate from Luhmann, but similar in important ways, Gayatri Spivak, in *An Aesthetic Education in the Era of Globalization* (2012), suggested that aesthetic education is the preparation of the imagination for epistemological work. 'Epistemological work' is the meaning process, and 'preparing the imagination' is the teaching and learning process that works with learners, often youth, to become 'aware' of the processes of imagination behind, or underneath, meaning.

In his 2009 book, *Framing Consciousness in Art*, Gregory Minissale suggested two processes of consciousness at work in art: a lower and higher order. In everyday life, the lower order is concerned with perception, while the higher order is interested in the meaning of the perceptions and of acting upon them. Minissale argued, much like Luhmann, that art frames these processes so that the viewer (in visual art) becomes aware of the act of perception, a process called reflexivity. Reflexivity occurs when a viewer recognizes that the viewer has recognized a frame that surrounds and separates 'a thing' from everyday life. This separation draws the viewer into a self-consciousness about the viewer's perception-meaning process. Perception as a lower-order consciousness usually just functions routinely in the basement of experience, then enters into higher-order consciousness. Suddenly and surprisingly, perception emerges from the shadows into the full light of consciousness. Consciousness and perception in an engagement with art gets locked in a recursive process where consciousness reflects on the act of perception, and perception feeds consciousness, consciousness reflects on this new information, and perception feeds these to consciousness. John Dewey called this the aesthetic experience, and Arnold Berleant, the aesthetic field. Why do humans do this? Why do we enjoy it? In what ways does this occur in other cultural groups? These are exciting questions, certainly. So it is a source of great disappointment that aesthetic education is limited to art appreciation.

AESTHETIC EDUCATION AS ART APPRECIATION

A great deal of aesthetic education in formal schooling, when it contends with aesthetics at all, continues to rely upon the disciplinary model. Sometimes this begins with an outright dismissal of aesthetic education in favor of art education. Many young people's first introduction to music education is a teacher writing symbols on a white board saying, "ta-ta-tete-ta, this is music." But of course this is not music, it is a form of literacy developed in the Western Art Music tradition as a social technology to communicate and store musical ideas. In this literary tradition, youth were trained to listen, to read, to perform, to dance to, and ultimately, to appreciate the beautiful. When this cultural group began to expand their sphere of influence, they brought with them art and aesthetic education. The problem is not aesthetics necessarily; in fact this is quite an important discovery. The problem is that Enlightenment-era Europeans mistook a cultural aesthetics for universal aesthetics. The study of the beautiful was not understood to be one expression of aesthetics, but the only approach to the study of perception-meaning. Europeans have art, and everyone else has generalized culture. In *The Darker Side of Western Modernity*, Walter Mignolo (2011) explained:

> That foundation was crucial in the sixteenth century, when European men and institutions began to populate the Americas, founding universities and establishing a system of knowledge, training Indians to paint churches and to legitimize artistic principles and practices that were connected with the symbolic in the control of authority and with the economic in the mutual complicity between economic wealth and the splendor of the arts. From the seventeenth century, European colonies provided the raw material for the foundation of museums of curiosities (Kunstkamera), which later on divided pieces from the non-European world (museums of natural history, of anthropology) from museums of art (primarily European, from the Renaissance on). (20–21)

This framework gets applied in all colonial situations. Authorities make it their mission to intercede into indigenous symbolic processes. Aesthetics and aesthetic education play a role in this, and continue to do so. From my perspective, that of a European Canadian male, I can see the continuation of cultural colonization at work in the century-long use of residential school education to "kill the Indian in the child", the practice of government supported cultural genocide. A photographic record of residential school musical bands shows generations of aboriginal youth playing concert band and wind band instruments, symbols of their cultural possession. Plato's observations on aesthetic education as discipline take a sinister turn. The pedagogy of Music appreciation, for instance, works to create young listeners who *appreciate* the masterworks of the dominator culture—youth willing to be disciplined as the "mark of an aesthetically prepared and culturally elevated individual" (Dell'Antonio, 2004, 3).

Terry Eagleton and Luc Ferry have pointed out that aesthetics is really about an Enlightenment conception of individual and/or personal development and bourgeoisie morality (as cited in Guyer, 2005, 30), and less about an inquiry into human practices of expression and reception. Walter Mignolo (2011) has argued that the very notion of Art, upon which Kant's aesthetics is based, is itself a social construction, used as a tool to establish hierarchies of expression that allowed European bourgeois expression to dominate the rest. This strategy elevated European cultural output and defined it as art, which thereby cast aspersions on the expressive practices of other cultural groups, terming them folklore, craft, popular culture, etc. Mignolo termed this technique colonial difference.

CULTURAL STUDIES OF SENSIBILITY AS CRITICAL PEDAGOGY

A critical aesthetic education begins with the cultural studies of sensibility. This requires that you and your students (or teachers) develop relationships with local arts practitioners 'to do' cultural studies together. I follow Handel Wright's (2003) assertion that cultural studies is more than theorizing, it is "the idea of articulating theory, empirical research, and service learning as interrelated elements of cultural studies work …cultural studies as social justice praxis" (p. 807). Wright suggested that we begin by "taking cultural studies personally" (p. 809), as an epistemological mission of sorts, dedicated to understanding our lives within our cultures, and our societies.

The work of documenting cultural aesthetics and then of building critical aesthetic education is only going to happen with a variety of partnerships. Moreover, it is through the developing of these partnerships—between professors, teachers, students, cultural aesthetic community members, government agencies, boards of education—that we begin to re-write and undo colonial difference. Critical Aesthetic Education, because of our colonial history, necessarily begins with recognizing the impact of colonization upon our imaginations. This is a personal commitment to decolonization that will help us develop the epistemological curiosity (Freire, 2001, p. 35) necessary for this difficult intellectual work. Taking cultural studies personally will help to build the type of imagination and/or consciousness necessary for rigorous critical work. As Freire (2001) wrote:

> To think correctly demands profundity and not superficiality in the comprehension and interpretation of the facts. It presupposes an openness that allows for the revision of conclusions; it recognizes not only the possibility of making a new choice or a new evaluation but also the right to do so. (p. 39)

I have suggested above that a place to begin is the deconstruction of the colonial difference, a starting point Freire (2001) would approve: "it is equally part of right thinking to reject decidedly any and every form of discrimination. Preconceptions of race, class, or sex offend the essence of human dignity and constitute a radical negation of democracy" (41). And it is with this concern for the development of epistemological curiosity that I conclude with three concerns that you might take up in your cultural studies of aesthetics.

THREE TOPICS FOR A CRITICAL PEDAGOGY OF POPULAR MUSIC

The first is a concern about the reification of culture. Even as I wrote about the Black Arts Movement foundations of Hiphop Kulture (in the coming chapters), I am self-conscious about participating in the cementing of a fixed historical narrative for a culture. Hiphop Kulture is constantly informed and constantly in flux. In the Hiphop Kulture community in Edmonton, Canada, where I live and work, there are a variety of histories, and a variety of staring points, that weave a richly textured and complex culture together. It is not homogeneous, nor even a single community. When I use the word, *culture*, I mean a symbolic learning network of individuals connected by shared communication. Culture is a learning system, and a system that learns, changes. When culture stops being a learning system it becomes a fixed form, a commodity, and stops being an engine of human development. Black culture in the Black Arts Movement is therefore different from the Black culture that Mark Anthony Neal 2002) discussed as the post-soul aesthetic:

> In the post-soul aesthetic I am surmising that there is an aesthetic centre within contemporary black popular culture that at various moments considers issues like deindustrialization, desegregation, the corporate annexation of black popular expression, cybernization in the workforce, the globalization of finance and communication, the general commodification of black life and culture, and the proliferation of black "meta-identities," while continuously collapsing on modern concepts of blackness and reanimating "Premodern" (African?) concepts of blackness. I am also suggesting that this aesthetic ultimately renders many 'traditional' tropes of blackness dated and even meaningless; in its borrowing from black modern traditions, it is so consumed with its contemporary existential concerns that such traditions are not just called into question but obliterated. (2–3)

A cultural studies of youth aesthetics and the formation of sensibility will have to maintain a focus on the dynamic qualities of culture and resist the reification of youth culture, race, sex, etc.

The second concern is what Tim Wise (2010) called post-racial liberalism, that he defined as a "rhetoric of racial transcendence and a public policy agenda of colorblind universalism" with

> adherents dating back at least forty years, and which emerged after the civil rights revolution had largely accomplished its immediate goals …and following several years of violent uprisings in urban centers thanks to frustration at the

slow pace of change—especially with regard to economic opportunity—some of the nation's scholars and public intellectuals began to turn against race-specific remedies for lingering social inequalities. Beginning in the late 1970s ... and extending through to the Obama campaign for presidency, post-racial liberalism has advocated a de-emphasis of racial discrimination and race-based remedies for inequality, in favor of class-based or "universal" programs of uplift: from job creation politics to better education funding to health care reform. (16)

Post-racial liberalism threatens to return us, perhaps ironically (but not humorously), to the very same enlightenment values that Walter Mignolo identified as the basis of colonial difference. As I have tried to show, universalism is a cover for cultural hegemony. Colourblind universalism is the dismissal of cultural diversity, the turning back of the gains we have made. What is left after post-racial liberalism is not an absence of culture, but a false cultural universalism, a singular identity by which to dismiss all others. A cultural studies of sensibility will need to grapple with communities of difference; how people can be together in community and in culture *and* also recognize their diversity.

Finally, my third concern, one already well documented in cultural studies, is the impact of neoliberal cultural production on local culture. Henry Giroux (2009) warned that, "in the society of consumers no one can become a subject without first turning into a commodity" (p. 31). The production of a cultural commodity transforms culture from a learning system into a thing. Cultural appreciation is based upon this fixed view of culture. Neoliberal cultural production changes the framework of cultural appreciation because of cultural value to cultural appreciation based on commodity success. Central to the concern about neoliberal cultural production is the impact that it has on individual consciousness. It has been shown, time and again, that these cultural commodities, produced for sale by the popular music industry, target young people to "deal with their lack of self-confidence, powerlessness, and the endless indignities heaped upon them in a consumer society" (Giroux, 2009, p. 59) by buying products produced by corporations "which use magnetic resonance images (MRI) to map brain patterns and reveal how consumers respond to advertisements or products" (Giroux, 2009, p. 59). This process is called neuromarketing, and it attests to precisely what Plato, Baumgarten, Arnold, and Adorno have suggested, a connection between aesthetics and consciousness.

Instead of working to elevate consciousness in pro-social ways, corporations tend to target and exploit weaknesses, often using ploys that tend towards the anti-social and anti-cultural. It is not their fault; their job is to produce consumers. Youth need critical aesthetic education, not in order to dismiss cultural production, but to 'critically' engage it. Educators need to make it our mission to provide youth the necessary skills to resist a very prepared and equipped sales machine working to create better consumers, not better people. Educators play a frontline role in working with youth to develop *conscientização*, the critical awareness necessary to simultaneously disempower mass marketing and support local cultural production. It is my contention that this cultural resistance is currently being practiced in youth cultures in your community. Instead of 'educated' adults telling youth how to resist, I would suggest making it an educational commitment to work with youth to document existing youth culture resistance movements happening right now in your community. This is cultural studies of aesthetics as aesthetics education.

NOTE

[1] Originally published as "Cultural Studies of Youth Culture: Aesthetics as Critical Aesthetics Education". In *Critical Youth Studies Reader*, Awad Ibrahim & Shirley R. Steinberg (Eds.), Peter Lang Publishing, New York, 2014, pp. 434–443. Reprinted with permission.

CRITICAL PEDAGOGY OF LISTENING

Practicing critical pedagogy calls teacher and student into confrontation with neoliberal popular culture. But what is less clear, from a disciplinary point of view, is how and where this confrontation takes places. This application of critical pedagogy in higher education music classrooms requires the development of disciplinary specific skill-sets and the development of a critical pedagogy of listening.

But this is not without challenges. In current practice students learn about popular music through historically oriented lectures focused on the birth, life, death, and works of great musicians. This approach, termed musicological, has been adopted from the teaching of Western Art Music (WAM) history. A second, sociological approach is used less frequently. The sociological approach developed in part from cultural studies focuses attention on issues of class, race, gender, desire, and space. In the sociological approach "the music" is used as a platform for sociological themes. What is common to these two approached is the often rudimentary approach to listening called music appreciation.

Music appreciation is a form of listening for non-musicians. Music appreciation was developed as an introduction to the history and development of Western Art Music. The goal was to introduce the sounds and structures of dominant classical music so that students would possess an "appreciation" of the "master works" of a dominant culture. This form of listening, called structural listening, asked students to memorize forms and often melodies checked with "drop the needle" tests where instructors would literally, in the days of vinyl records, drop the need on the track and students would be asked to identify the composer, the title of the piece, and often the movement. In this way the student could be introduced to Western Art Music structures and be expected to memorize the canon for later recall.

Applying music appreciation pedagogy to popular music and popular culture studies has not yet been problematized. Critical Pedagogy of Music is incommensurate with music appreciation, as I will show. This creates a methodological vacuum that must be addressed. The second half of the article provides a pedagogical contribution I call critical listening.

PART ONE: FROM MUSIC EDUCATION TO A CRITICAL PEDAGOGY FOR POPULAR MUSIC

Music Appreciation

The impulse to teach youth to appreciate Western Art Music is an extension of Matthew Arnold's idea of culture as the best of what has been written and performed

(Arnold, 1869). Culture, in this case the enlightenment culture of the land owning class, was collected, codified, and celebrated by the institutions founded and funded by them. This is the political elite whose rise to independence from aristocracy and papacy took a long road to democracy. The development and defense of democracy required the education of the masses. Education became a mission that mixed poorly with the uncritical acceptance of power won by violent revolution over already globalized colonial powers. This new revolutionary land owning and merchant class entered into an education project that simultaneously educated and colonized. The cultural output of these classes, coupled with what they could reclaim from the enlightenment, provided a platform for a claim to legitimacy. The previous ruling class claimed divine authority for its kings and the priests. The new ruling class, as Zygmut Bauman (1982) has noted simultaneously created and policed "the people" into existence. The people were educated in the image of the ruling class as a strategy to ensure its legitimacy and continuation. A small part of this cultural education was musical. Educating "the people" about the inherent value of the music of the new ruling class, what became known as western art music (WAM), became a priority.

Enlightenment cultural education began as the utopian dream of radical revolutionaries and its practitioners still retain, to some extent, imprints of these progressive dreams. In Joseph Kerman's 10th edition of Listen (Kerman, 2008) he writes: "if we do not understand the past, we are only doomed to living in the present" (Kerman, 2008, xiii). Kerman's narrative of unproblematic progress begins in the "first millennium C.I., European culture was the culture of Christianity" regardless of the number of indigenous, Jewish, and Islamic cultures (to name only the most obvious) who could claim otherwise. The discourse quickly turns to and remains focused on literacy:

> Around 1100, music manuscripts of a new kind began to appear—often richly illuminated manuscripts, transmitting music composed for princely courts, as well as music for the Church. Slowly the Church was yielding power to kings and nobles. Courts furnished the locale for instrumental and vocal music for many centuries. Music was now entertainment for court society. (ibid)

Public opera houses and concert halls were built, while in the background, court power declined. Concert music, it is said, became available to all, at least to those who "could afford it" or were the "well-to-do". The class dimensions of music performance and the introduction of entrepreneurship within a developing musical class are left unstated. In the following paragraph Kerman makes a grand leap in his teleological account of musical development, "Meanwhile European music took a big leap to Latin America and then to North America—first in the California missions and then in the English colonies. In the twentieth century it also became a major presence in Japan and other non-European countries" (Kerman, 2008, xiv–xv).

The historical development of "music"—no mention is even made of WAM being one of many competing musical systems existing simultaneously even in Europe let alone everywhere else—gets condensed to the worldwide expansion of WAM's literate tradition. The teaching of Western Art Music is a practice of colonization. Here Kerman shows that the point of reciting the history and development of Western Art Music is not to understand a complex history but to celebrate the wonder of its expansion. The military power of colonization and the cultural imperialism (Battiste, 2013) of music education is erased:

> In the sixteenth century, when European men and institutions began to populate the Americas, founding universities and establishing a system of knowledge, training Indians to paint churches and to legitimize artistic principles and practices that were connected with the symbolic in the control of authority and with the economic in the mutual complicity between economic wealth and the splendor of the arts. (Mignolo, 2011, 20)

WAM is taught to "civilize" and inspire cultural awe in the uninitiated. The student is left with the impression that WAM has been already embraced by a world of listeners who were waiting to warmly welcome all cultural newcomers with open arms, once they learn to "appreciate" the inherent cultural value of its forms:

> The basic activity that leads to the love of music and to its understanding—to what is sometimes called "music appreciation"—is listening to particular pieces of music again and again...These discussion are meant to introduce you to the contents of these works and their aesthetic qualities: what goes on in the music, and how it affects us. (Kerman, 2008, 3)

In other similar texts critical interrogation of WAM is often headed off very quickly: "Though there is a vast amount of fascinating and valuable biographical and historical information available about music, I believe the core of great listening has less to do with facts and far more to do with our ability to pay attention, listen closely, and notice" (Kapilow, 2008, 3).

Musicians who are not trained in the WAM system are often left out of the discussion entirely or, when included, tend to be either ridiculed or presented in such a way as to suggest their importance is culturally marginal:

> Our purpose is to expand the listening experience through a heightened awareness of many styles of music, including those representing various subculture of the American population. We will hear the uniquely American forms of ragtime, blues, jazz, and musical theater, as well as rock and contemporary world music. The book seeks to place music, whether art, tradition, or popular, within its cultural context, and to highlight the relationships between different styles. (Forney, 2007, 3)

Contrary to the authors stated intention "popular styles" get only very cursory coverage from page 550–595 (45 pages!) of a 677 page text. The lesson is that "low-culture" requires only a very cursory introduction and that "high culture," weighed in the number of pages, is much richer, more complex, and requires much greater study and reflection. This is a compelling strategy and one has continued to do the ideological work of furthering WAM enlightenment culture, the expressive culture or European landowners, into the future.

Music Appreciation in a Neoliberal Age

Popular music courses were introduced into the university classroom, separate from, but on the wave of social change. After many years of debate about the cultural worth of popular music and jazz it seems that, for many schools, it was the arrival of the globalized music industry and the rise of neoliberalism that helped finally convince faculties of the usefulness of these courses. A small publishing industry soon emerged with new popular music texts offered each year and pushed upon new instructors trying to cope with swelling enrollments. Central to nearly all of these texts was music appreciation, but this time with a twist. CD packages, which had been developed for WAM texts, quickly gave way to downloadable song lists, sold separately from iTunes. Publishers rapidly developed links with the popular music industry and the music industry found a way into the ears of a new and captive audience.

There is a short distance from music appreciation to the education of students for music consumption. It seems that the liberal dream of cultural development by music appreciation has become a cover for the sale of music downloads to students. Currently there is no research project of any size that has looked into this issue so I will generalize from my experience of teaching one such course over the last seven years and triangulate this position with conversations I have had with fellow popular music instructors. In many cases well-intentioned instructors, many of whom are grad students, postdocs, or sessionals have little time to reflect on the pedagogical implications of turning their classrooms into an outlet for iTunes and Apple Inc. These instructors, myself included, often building on their experience with music appreciation are likely to see a suggested song list as a natural, unproblematic, and perhaps necessary aspect of a popular music pedagogy. Transferring this methodology seems sensible and even laudable. But this approach has, quite unintentionally I think, replaced Arnold's dream of enlightenment-advancement-through-cultural with something else, that industry creates culture. A survey of current popular music history texts illustrates this point. Popular music pedagogy has limited the discussion of music culture to a history of successfully produced cultural products manufactured and aggressively marketed by the popular music industry for mass consumption.

Henry Giroux warns that, "in the society of consumers no one can become a subject without first turning into a commodity" (Giroux, 2009, 31). It is this subject, the very one that is produced for sale by the popular music industry, that targets young people to "deal with their lack of self-confidence, powerlessness, and the endless indignities heaped upon them in a consumer society" (ibid, 59). Producing subjects for the popular music industry is big business employing specialists of all kinds to aid in the sale of manufactured pop culture to young people. Helping to provide ready-made songlists to over-worked instructors is an easy solution and much less complex than the "neuromarketing which uses magnetic resonance images (MRI) to map brain patterns and reveal how consumers respond to advertisements or products" (ibid, 59). It is within this ecology of influence that music appreciation is now nested. As an opening move to interrogate music appreciation as a methodology for teaching popular music within a neoliberal age I have turned to Critical Pedagogy to help develop critical awareness, for myself, and for my students.

PART TWO: CRITICAL PEDAGOGIES FOR MUSIC EDUCATION

Critical Pedagogy

Paulo Freire, echoed by contemporary critical pedagogues, accused liberal arts education of developing a banking approach to education in which students are "receptacles to be filled by the teacher" (1970, 53). In this model, the student becomes a passive consumer of a performance. Passivity and quietness are counter democratic, every democratic citizen must have a voice (hooks, 2010, 55–56) because "human existence cannot be silent" (Freire, 1970, 69). Critical pedagogy acknowledges that a democratic citizenry requires agency and that this must be taught in school. Engaged citizenship cannot be developed in students who are trained to sit and passively consume information. Students need to be taught to speak to power, but they also need to be taught to listen critically to the voices of power. Being able to critically engage the messages that are received in a world that is being made good for business and bad for democracy is simply central to the development of real democratic institutions. But it would be naïve to suggest that one just has to flip an imaginary critical switch or expect our students to develop critical consciousness themselves by writing papers and learning to hear and recognize the structure of songs in "drop by needle" tests.

Students enter university are already enrolled in competing education programs. Giroux, drawing from the observations of Stuart Hall, argued that popular culture "redefines the politics of power, the political nature of representation, and the centrality of pedagogy as a defining principle of social change" (Giroux, 2000, 354). Contemporary students are engaged in two contradictory programs. The first is partially under our control. It is the liberal arts education that has long been recognized as the foundation of democratic citizenship (Dewey, 1916) even if it is also tainted by its complicity in colonialism. The second, outside our influence, is the spectacle of media and the political and educational forces of corporate neoliberal globalization. Cultural studies scholars from the Frankfurt School (Adorno, Horkeimer, Benjamin, Marcuse) to the present day acknowledge the anti-democratic tendencies of popular culture and its role in the advance of neoliberalism (Harvey, 2005) as the "ideology of imperialist white-supremacist capitalist patriarchy" (hooks, 2003, 11). The development of critical pedagogy (Friere, 1970, 1998; McLaren, 1998, 2007; Giroux, 1997, 2009) has emerged alongside cultural studies (Giroux, 2000; Mallot, 2004; Roy, 2003) as an attempt to develop a program of classroom critical engagement with popular culture (Daspit, 1999), a dialectical and, indeed, dialogical engagement between the "official" school pedagogy and public pedagogy, the teaching function of industrial popular culture.

Critical community oriented pedagogy, in opposition to dominating public pedagogy, is built upon the understanding that "the education of the public occurs in public" (Pinar, 2010, xv). Public pedagogues from W.E.B. Dubois and Franz Fanon, to Paulo Freire, bell hooks, Henry Giroux, Peter McLaren, Joe Kincheloe and Shirley Steinberg understand that urban cultural practices happening in local neighborhoods are central to the education of citizens. Education practice that happens in school must be able to be applied to the real lives of our students. It is essential that the skills we teach contribute positively to the confrontation students have with public consumer pedagogy. This means we must teach methods that allow students to confront popular culture themselves and in community.

Community art practice plays an important role in this regard: "an artist's lyrics and music intertwine to create passion, rage, and action, where before there was only overwhelming alienation and acquiescence" (Sandlin, 2010, 1). It has been noted, for instance, that in Hiphop culture "the mentor-apprentice relationship ... raises the graffiti crew from mere association of writers to educational organization that deliberately and systematically transmit knowledge, skills, values, and sensibilities to their members" (Christen, 2010, 235; Cremin, 1988). When these skills confront the dominant classist, sexist, racist, and colonial discourses so common in popular media, a subjective conflict emerges. Critical postcolonial public pedagogues realize that:

> The dynamic psychological and emotional structures that shape our subjectivity (our empathetic intelligence, ways of seeing, sense of integrity, community and identity) are acquired (often very violently) in our most intensely charged intimate and public relationships. For these reasons their origins tend to be deeply hidden from ourselves and they seem inexplicable and unchangeable. But they dynamically permeate all the spaces in our micro-social relations because they are inscribed within our bodies, in our very presence. (Cohen, 2005, 195)

Critical pedagogues want to promote this confrontation and empower our students to live rich democratic lives. For this to occur we must train our students to confront popular culture in a critical fashion by moving past rote learning about popular music history and passive listening. Our students need to learn to confront the messages they hear, the one that they currently mostly accept.

Towards Critical Listening

Currently, listening in music education is divided between structural listening and music appreciation. Structural listening encourages students to learn forms, melodies, and harmonic developments of works. Music appreciation is shorthand for musicological listening best suited for non-musicians. Music appreciation, as discussed above, was created to help new listeners appreciate the master works of a dominant culture. These two approaches have led to a "neglect of structures relatable to music's role in society as a symbolic system" (Tagg, 1992, 1) and as Ruth Subotinik has pointed out, the "listener" that is imagined in both instances is willing to be disciplined as the "mark of an aesthetically prepared and culturally elevated individual" (Dell'Antonio, 2004, 3). I wish to be clear at this juncture that I am not following Adorno down well-worn paths of cultural elitism vis-à-vis the culture industry (Adorno, 2001). It is not elitist to argue that education should teach democracy and critical evaluation over blind acceptance of cultural value produced by cultural industries. But as I have tried to make clear above, this is difficult in music because WAM music appreciation is based on exactly this form of uncritical acceptance of cultural value. Music education has moved from training listeners to accept WAM to training listeners to accept Popular Music. It is simply a shift of masters. The way out of this dilemma is to create a critical form of listening, not exactly undisciplined, but perhaps obstreperous.

Replacing disciplined listening with obstreperous/critical listening might begin with a sociological approach to listening which attempts to find how social meaning in music is "located in its function as a social symbol" (Shepherd, 1991, 13). This is quite a challenge because as Philip Tagg has pointed out, the lack of research about "music's role in society as a symbolic system" (1) puts the music analyst in the unenviable position to both figure out (a) what music structures are relevant but also (b) how they work. My solution for Tagg's dilemma is to make this the core of a pedagogical model for listening. Following Freire's idea that a critical student will learn only through their interrogation of the social world, critical listening is a model for exploratory, obstreperous listeners who are training to be musical cultural analysts instead of disciplined music appreciators.

Overview of Foundations of Critical Listening

The challenge for critical listening pedagogy is to make the practically invisible social process of meaning creation-and-sharing in music explicit for both instructors and students. This method will begin at a structural level. Critical listening should not dismiss the existence and importance of music structures but instead, will not expect musical structure to be self-explanatory. I draw upon Adorno's ideas of import and function from Aesthetic Theory (1997), as a way of thinking about the dual analytical process which works towards collapsing together an analysis of music structures (i.e. melody, rhythm, tone, structure) with an analysis of social and cultural circulation (i.e.audio and visual medium, performance venue). Music structures become sound-grammars encoded with socially informed meaning which I will call codes, a rich resource for a semiotically informed music analysis. This might usefully be seen as an auditory equivalent of the text-based semiotic process espoused by cultural studies currently.

The leap from musical structure to codes and therefore semiotic analysis is not as large as might first be suspected. One explanation for the process by which sound-grammars are converted to codes is called audiation (Gordon, 1997). Gordon suggests that by listening a student learns the "logic" of musical flows and learns to follow where music is leading. It seems that audiation works by a process of normalization, or sound habit, which has much of what Bourdieu suggested with his concept of habitus. Audiation is also helpful because (a) it is a listener oriented approach to music education and (b) it is easily testable. It is possible to play a series of notes for a student and ask them to provide a "logical" next note. But while this does test a certain kind of listening knowledge, it is a culturally embedded one which does not explain what these melodies might "mean," and from an epistemological perspective, how we might come to know these meanings. Audiation therefore does not provide us with what we need.

An alternative example is Eric Clarke's notion of ecological listening (2005) that draws upon J.J. Gibson's notion of affordance to explain how "the human observer learns to detect what have been called the values or meaning of things, perceiving their distinctive features, putting them into categories and subcategories..." (37). Ecological listening is a valuable idea because it focuses on perception and "emphasizes the perceiving organism's adaptation to its environment, and the manner in which perceptual information specifies events in the world" (ibid. 154). Ecological listening includes audiation and social perception but lacks a needed historical dimension. Clarke, who is coming from a music psychology perspective, is interested in how a listener processes data. I am interested in including audiation and affordance as first steps in understanding how listeners inherit and normalize music codes in the production of their symbolic musical habitus, a multimodal discourse that produces a style community.

Critical Listening Codes and Democratic Engagement

Zygmunt Bauman argues that "critical reflection is the essence of all genuine politics" (1999, 84) and requires what Cornelius Castoriadis called "the discovery and explicit admission of the inescapably human origin of human institutions" which requires "collective responsibility for their merits and deficiencies" (80). Critical reflection accordingly requires that we recognize and assert our autonomy as agents in the creation and preservation of social networks. Critical thinking emerges, in part, from the act of critique which presents both the past and the future as "uncertain, unfinished, incomplete and open to re-examination" (85).

My interest is to suggest one new way to approach critical thinking about music, in a way that utilizes an inherently musical process, listening. To do this I have drawn from four different models that use semiotics. I have chosen to focus on semiotics because musical meaning seems to function in a semiotic way, that is, musical sounds, like words in a language, are encoded with meaning in complex social processes. These processes occur within a symbolic register and semiotics seems to be the best model for discussing the construction, maintenance, and social function of these symbols. One of the downsides of semiotics, as it currently exists, is that musical ideas do not have direct symbolic associations the way language does. But while this may be true, I do not have any interest in developing a dictionary or encyclopedia of sound-grammars which may be universally applied to listening. I am interested in suggesting a method for discussing how meaning is produced within localized social groups, following Joe Kincheloe, a critical constructivism of listening where processes of confrontation and negotiation of sound produce shared meaning within local communities.

Another potential difficulty that semiotics poses critical listening is its value in discussing emotional registers of music listening. Semiotics is very good at pointing to concepts but what about desires? Desires are difficult to assign to specific symbolic print codes. While this is true there is no reason why this objection might deny that desires can become associated with aural codes than can be heard. Desires like longing, sexual desire, violence, nostalgia may be even easier to identify in listening than in print media. The rest of this article will trace a line through semiotic discourse to illustrate the semiotic basis for critical listening which will include (a) Peirce and Saussure's basic idea of the sign and code as a starting point (b) Jean-Jacques Nattiez and Philip Tagg's models of music semiotics (c) Jean Baudrillard's model of critical semiotics, and (d) Paulo Freire's culture circle model of literacy education, the core of critical pedagogy, which uses deconstructed semiotics as its main pedagogical technique. The article will conclude with the beginning of a semiotics of sound, informed by critical pedagogy, and an example of critical listening at work.

PART THREE: CRITICAL SEMIOTICS OF LISTENING

Semiotics

Semiotics has a long and complex history. It is enough to say that I build upon the central notion of Ferdinand de Saussure and Charles Sander's Pierce that a sign is the unification of the signifier and the signified. From a music perspective the signifier is the sound-code which becomes connected to a social fact, the signified, which then becomes a sign. Semiotics has played an important role in communication studies and in critical and social theory especially in the work of Stuart Hall. The noted Canadian communication scholar Marshall McLuhan wrote in The Gutenburg Galaxy (1962) that "from the meaningless sign attached to the meaningless sounds we have built the shape and meaning of western man" (50). Reverse engineering this connection will allow the analyst to identify how values and meanings get attached to signs. This approach has been well used in the analysis of print media but has found only limited support in music analysis.

Music Semiotics

Music semiotics has taken two main forms. The first was suggested by Jean-Jacques Nattiez who built upon Saussure in Music and Discourse: Towards a Semiology of Music (1990). I began reading this book with great interest but then, deep in a discussion about a semiotic discourse of music, I began to loose sight of an application. Nattiez is heroic in his attempt to provide a semiotic foundation for music analysis but he does not produce a method which might compare to what has been done in British cultural studies. Nattiez suggests that "musical semiology thus touches upon this "transcendental" dimension, present in all manner of musical analysis. Precisely because semiology is concerned with all symbolic forms, it can put its finger on an aspect of the problem that few musicologists…have thematicized explicitly" (Nattiez, 1990, 174). However, he provides little in the way of a tool box to illustrate how one might go forward to teach students how to practice music semiotics and how, as a researcher, I might begin applying semiotic research with a eye towards producing code inventories as they are produced in listener and producer communities.

A second approach was developed by Philip Tagg and is somewhat different because he describes music semiotics as "the relations between the sounds we call musical and what those sounds signify to those producing and hearing the sounds in specific sociocultural contexts" (2012, 91). Tagg attepts to make clear a distinction between theoretical systems or syntax, semantics, and pragmatics and in doing so does not choose to focus exclusively on European Art Music, the way Nattiez and other music semioticians have (Tagg, 1987, 4). Music semiotics, Tagg suggests, could be subdivided into music syntax (the systems of relations between signs in formal structures), music semantics (the relationship between signs and their relationships to the signified) and music pragmatics (the relations between signs and the impact they have on the people who use them). Tagg suggests semantic and pragmatic studies in music-semiotics have been slow to develop because a semiotic theory has emerged from literary oriented scholarship (2012, 92) which is more interested in syntax. A difficulty a listening oriented music-semiotics must face is the lack of research on aural semiotic codes. Tagg suggests the need for a music-semiotics that challenges the "grapho-centrism and the absolutist aesthetics of music in official institutions of education and research in the west". One of the ways of undertaking this is a listening oriented pragmatic semiotics, that is, research in how sound codes are organized and shared between listeners who use them. For reasons unclear to me, Tagg does not draw connections between his suggestions and critical semiotics. My suggestion for critical listening does just this, mixes pragmatic semiotics of music with critical semiotics and critical pedagogy.

Critical Semiotics

A periodization of critical semiotics might identify its origin at Marx's deconstruction of the commodity form. In his discussion of the commodity form he was able to show that what appears to be a commodity with a sensible price is really a complex expression of social value. Value, Marx argued, is really two different things that are collapsed together, use-value and exchange-value. There is no essential value of a commodity because money expresses value (use+exchange) itself and obscures that it really is a stand-in for social ideas about labour (concrete and abstract labour exchanged in relative and equivalent forms). Marx argued that deconstructing the commodity form opens a window into the study of society.

While this description overly simplifies Marx's offering it is helpful to point to the implicit role of semiotics in Marx's thought and the streams of thought that would build upon this aspect of his work in critical theory. I draw upon two critical theorists who, I think, provide a framework for critical music semiotics, both inspired by Marx, and who have informed cultural studies. The first is, perhaps unsurprisingly, Theodor W. Adorno, and the second is Jean Baudrillard.

Adorno

Adorno, especially in Aesthetic Theory, provides a general analytical framework for a sociological study of music, which I suggest, provides an important link between pragmatist semiotics and sociology. Adorno suggests that the analysis of a musical work can be examined in two-part motion, the first Import, and the second, function. Import is a close reading of the music work which requires a hermeneutic analysis of the content and form of the work. The second phase, function, requires that we examine the political and economic circulation of the work to see the ways production, distribution/exchange, and consumption impacts aesthetic meaning. Adorno himself does not provide a useful example of this analysis on popular music, because of his general distaste for it borne from his elitism. Nor does he provide us with an example of its use in aural analysis because generally "Adorno was out of touch with the musical habits of the populace" (Tagg, 2012, 85) which were and still are overwhelmingly aural and because of Adorno's aversion to musics somatic (bodily-emotional-physical) power (ibid).

Criticisms aside, I can take Marx's analysis of the commodity form without also accepting Marx's belief in linear history or in the dictatorship of the proletariat. So I can take from Adorno his sociological approach to aesthetics without his elitism. Carrying these threads forward I will add one more analytical piece derived from the critical semiotics of Jean Baudrillard.

Baudrillard

In Baudrillard's For a Critique of a Political Economy of the Sign (1981) he reaches back and expands upon Marx's discourse on the commodity. Marx lived in a world of strict class lines. The commodity form that Marx discussed was marked by the social world about which he theorized. Baudrillard expands upon Marx's ideas of use-value and exchange-value and introduces symbolic-value. Through symbolic-value

Baudrillard is able to return to the logic of Marx, the commodity form as a window to the social world, but in an expanded anthropological and semiotically informed way.

Baudrillard began this line of thinking as a student of Henri Lefebvre, who himself was interested in using semiological categories to expand the analytical power of Marxism for a sociological analysis of everyday life. Lefevre contended that advanced capitalism spread its oppressive tentacles beyond the workplace to the world of leisure and the family" (Poster, 1979, 280). Baudrillard, building upon Lefebvre, returned to and dismissed Marx in his critique. He returned to Marx's rigour but rejected Marx's understanding of the commodity, and Marx's dismissal of the negative aspects of consumption (the fetish). Instead of being moral about consumption, Baudrillard argues, we should study the roles consumed objects play in the structuring of social life. From this observation, that the consumption of objects is always the exchange of social, we can return to Adorno's aesthetic theory and recognize that within function lies the symbolic-exchange, which has already collapsed with the Import. This observation illustrates that all so-called hermeneutic analysis is also a specific kind of social analysis, because all previous learning, which is the frame by which culture analysis occurs, was born of a specific social location. The next step is to create a system to teach this analytic form. For this I turn to Paulo Freire's culture circles and critical pedagogy, where, to my surprise, I found another example of critical semiotics at work.

CRITICAL PEDAGOGY AND CONSCIOUSNESS RAISING

In Freire's Education for Critical Consciousness (1974/2010), he makes a distinction between naïve consciousness and critical consciousness. Naïve consciousness "simply apprehends facts and attributes them a superior power by which it is controlled and to which it must therefore submit ... resigned to the impossibility of resisting the power of facts" (39). Critical consciousness, on the other hand, "is integrated with reality" (39). To be integrated into reality means to have a dialogical relationship with the production of reality. This stance puts the power to construct one's own reality directly within her or his power. The act of confronting reality will lead, Freire asserts, to the development of a standoff between the way things are and the way they could be. It will subsequently lead to a standoff between the powers that construct reality in their image and the image of the world of the oppressed. The power of critical awareness emerges when the oppressed realize they have the power to change their reality. This awareness leads to the transformation of the oppressed into a conscious community willing to work together with a clear focus on what needs to be done to make their community better.

It is, indeed, towards world transformation that Freire encourages. It is a humble revolution built upon very small steps. Freire presented each culture circle as a "situation." The goal was not to show people that they are not powerful, that would not be helpful at all. It would only add to the already oppressive feeling of powerlessness that is already engendered through public pedagogy. The "situations" at hand would become the social levers to aid in the development of the participants' conscientization, or the becoming of critical consciousness, as discussed above.

To do this he taught literacy. But instead of bringing in teaching books and primers, which would teach literacy but not empowerment, he worked with a visual artist to draw situations familiar to his non-literate students. The students would discuss the situation presented in the drawing and would begin, phonetically, to compile a written vocabulary based on their specific cultural contexts. In this way, Freire suggested, students would learn that literacy emerges from culture, and therefore literacy might emerge from any culture, not just the culture of the oppressors. Freire's model of critical pedagogy put the student in a position of social researcher and does what Zygmunt Bauman urges of politics, to illustrates that the past, present, and future are social and cultural constructions produced by people participating in social formation, distribution, and maintenance.

Critical Music Semiotics: Critical Listening

Freire's project, upon which Critical Pedagogy has formed, provides two things, (a) a pedagogical context from which to draw guidance and (b) another example of the type of critical semiotics I have been discussing above. While not widely discussed, the similarities between Freire's method and critical semiotics is worth noting. He illustrates that the sign (the written word) is the combination of an action or thing (signified) and the utterance that stands in for it (signifier). Freire's critical pedagogy has, at its root the same interests as critical semiotics, that is, to identify the sign and open it up to illustrate how it is socially produced. Critical listening can now be asserted as the joining of three streams: critical semiotics, music semiotics, and critical pedagogy.

Musical sounds get invested by meaning as they are interpreted, used, marketed, distributed, and shared by people and groups in the social world. Musical sounds are conceptually rich and are used by composers and sound designers to evoke associations. Listeners who have learned to form the same socio-musical connections share these associations. We are confronted here by three interconnected questions (a) how do these code associations form, (b) how are they learned, (c) how can they be studied. The solution for these three questions, as suggested above, is to use critical listening to deconstruct these connections and to then track down their historical formation. For instance, It is widely acknowledged that when Elvis was first played on the radio his "race" was unknown. But it is less widely discussed that in order for there to be any confusion there first has to be a socially accepted "sound" of whiteness and blackness in American aural culture. Elvis' initial recording was successful because it playfully blurred the already accepted aural boundaries of race in America. Elvis presents a point of entry into the questions of aural-race formation which can then be deconstructed. The point is not to find the answer to why Elvis sounded white or black but to point out instead how certain sounds get mapped onto a socially constructed idea of race in the first place. Josh Kun's important work

Audiotopia (2005) does this by illustrating how race is formed in the American aural imagination. But if race, for instance, is so well articulated what else is?

Critical listening requires a starting point. Just as Marx chose the commodity form as his starting point, I will suggest sociological categories of class, ethnicity, gender, and sexuality as a starting point for critical listening. Students are asked to listen to their music and identify the ways race and ethnicity becomes associated with particular tones and sounds. In this process new ideas and sound codes will emerge. For instance, how twin ideas of ethnic orientalism and European rationalism get mapped onto the timbre of "sound" instruments over that of percussive "noise" instruments, like drums. Rationalism becomes marked by tonality and irrationalism by the pulse of drums, which then in many cases gets demarcated along moral lines of good (reality or rationalism) and bad (fantasy or irrationalism). When these ideas get mapped onto musical styles emerging from ethnic communities they form the basis of racial distinctions which follow along the lines of the ethnically identified power hierarchies which has the most "white" at the top and least "white" at the bottom. Connections form between these sound markers that allow for a number of non-similar and even antagonistic connections to be held in place like constellations. So a phrase from an orchestral string section might reference rationalism, heroicism, strength, and valour or it might represent colonialism, paternalism, and oppression. These ideas become evident everywhere. One might attempt an in-class analysis of a song like Part of Your World from Walt Disney's very successful The Little Mermaid (1989).

CRITICAL LISTENING APPLIED

Ariel the hero in Disney's retelling of The Little Mermaid, originally written in the early 19th century by Hans Christian Anderson with a remarkably different ending (spoiler alert—she dies), broods in her underwater secret hiding spot. She is a princess of a vast underwater territory with great wealth but she still wants more. Specifically, she wants the things that other people have in a near-mythical land far away. The soft strains of violins, wind instruments, and harp support Ariel as she sings about all the items she currently has in her collection but that: "who cares/no big deal/I want more". Ariel's longing is supported by long, elegant string phrases. A structural analysis of the piece would uncover little of musical interest. But it is how these unremarkable musical structures get mapped onto ideas of over-consumption, greed, and colonialism, that the musical choices become interesting. Ariel's song becomes a lament of "white" people who have "everything" but chase after new desire. The string theme draws on notions of elegance and station, which is of course precisely what a Disney princess, even an underwater one, possesses. And like many Disney princesses they also must have youth, charisma, femininity, and refinement, all aspects of bourgeois feminine power. The tonality of the strings recall the sophistication and station of WAM boosters and position Ariel within a European cultural lineage. It might be expected that from a North American perspective European cultural products, especially historical ones, recall high culture dominance and assists in asserting Ariel's royal station.

When these cultural ideas are married to the over-consumption message in the song's lyrics this children's entertainment takes on a different tone. The plaintive pop inflected strains of a young female character wanting something more than she currently has, a message that at its core is probably nearly universal, may also be coded as a destructive and spoiled material privileged youth who no longer knows how to appreciate abundance and instead feels a righteous obligation to everything. It is quite clear by the ending of the song Ariel will somehow plot her way to get what she desires, and, by the time the story ends, we discover that she will have had it all with no long-term consequence. The singing and naïve beauty of the strings support the growing contradiction of a destructive and morally ugly beauty. Already this critique poses difficult questions about the formation of cultural beauty and desire. How can a sound remain beautiful even as it clearly identifies a colonial and destructive heritage that is a root cause of global environmental change? European colonialism and contemporary western out-of-control consumption gets recast in Ariel as childish and unproblematic desire for the beautiful ornaments and cultural practices of others. This telling of the tale is drastically, and nearly perversely different from the original Anderson telling wherein the mermaid had to give up a great deal to have a chance to possess her desire, which in the end was ultimately denied.

CONCLUSION

Critical listening to Disney's *Part of Your World* illustrates the type of analysis that may emerge. This specific analysis opened a window to a discussion about the ways we value consumption and ownership and how we learn about what type of desires are socially supported and which kinds are warned about. A critical listening analysis provides the opportunity to discuss important social issues and creates a Freirian situation for students who might begin to contend with social codes that inform their social world. By recognizing The Little Mermaid as an example of public pedagogy the student might begin to think about the ways musical sounds situate class position and the way notions of beauty, may they be physical or musical, inform developing ideas of aesthetics for children and what these impacts might be. This example, or many others like it, might call childhood cultural products into question and create an environment for the development of critical thinking. Assisting students to critically engage with their aesthetic development will recall the core enlightenment interests so important to Mathew Arnold while avoiding the critical stunting which occurs when students are told to uncritical accept cultural products of supposed cultural value.

SECTION II

CASE STUDIES IN HIPHOP KULTURE

HIHOP CITIZEN[1]

Keepin' It Local

"Hip-hop culture," I say assertively to my introductory music class, "radically impacted the music industry by replacing a choice between Tin Pan Alley[2] products with a choice to participate in the making of an urban culture." Each year I reach this moment in the semester full of hope. I share with my students a wide variety of hip-hop styles from old school, gangsta rap, and raggaeton. The range of students' responses to the aforementioned hip-hop manifestations range from indifference to appreciation, but "keepin' it real" is a style this is important to all (Rose, 1994; Williams, 2010, p. 221). This focus on "keepin' it real" emphasizes urban authenticity through a connection to neighborhood. Community solidarity, therefore, is central to this type of hip-hop aesthetics.

But, in the fall of 2010, I began to wonder if this assumption is correct based upon the changing landscape of the music industry and the changing dynamics in the wider society. While it is true that hip-hop emerged during the decline of both the civil rights and Black Power movement and carried these messages forward, recently hip-hop has become "co-opted by the capitalistic, market-driven forces in society" (Williams, 2010, 221). Hip-hop has, in other words, become a global music commodity (Becker, Crawford, & Miller, 2002; Forman, 2000; Gilroy, 1993; Henderson, 1996; Ibrahim, 1999; Mitchell, 2001; Rose, 1994; Schloss, 2009) and is "dominated by commercialized, hegemonic popular culture" (Giroux, 2004; Williams, 2010). Therefore, I wanted to unearth whether there remains elements of Hiphop Kulture that have been able to resist the forces of Tin Pan Alley commoditization.

While I was mulling over this question, I became involved in an urban revitalization project in Edmonton, the capital city of oil rich Alberta. The 118-Avenue neighborhood is an older community in Edmonton which has, because of rising crime, been labeled "distressed". Distressed, of course, is a euphemism for a crime-ridden community lost to drugs and prostitution. But "distressed" communities also have lower real estate costs. In an expensive city like Edmonton, this often proves to be an important draw for artists. As an ethnomusicologist of popular music interested in urban music ecology, I was concerned about the cultural/artistic ecology of this community in the throes of gentrification. Unfortunately, I had little knowledge of the neighborhood; therefore, I contacted a few colleagues who are involved in the arts and were involved in projects in this area. Together we set up a series of meetings with young artists and presenters in the area.

The purpose of this chapter is to capture my involvement with the young artists and presenters who are involved in emancipatory forms of hip-hop in Edmonton. The first part of the chapter documents how I became connected with the research partners in this project and an overview of some of the obstacles inhibiting the hip-hop community in Edmonton and impoverished sections of Edmonton. Next, I highlight how we became aware of how neoliberalism is responsible for inhibiting the development of the hip-hop scene in Edmonton as well as the development of 118 Ave. Third, I flesh out how the research team formulated a research methodology and pedagogy to revitalize the hip-hop scene in Edmonton and our urban community itself. Finally, I suggest how this project impacted the individual members of the research team, the hip-hop community and this urban context. At the same time, I also highlight some of the obstacles of sustaining a cultural ecology that has the potential to raise critical awareness, inside and outside of the hip-hop world, of what causes oppression and how to dismantle it.

THE 118 AVE. MEETINGS AND HIP HOP ECOLOGY

In the fall of 2010, I attended a first meeting with a group who would become my research partners. It was arranged at a 118 Avenue theatre aptly named *The Avenue Theatre.* The theatre had recently come under the ownership of few young entrepreneurs who were working to create a not-for-profit foundation to support the theatre. Andrew, one of the owners, agreed to host this first meeting. I arrived to a cozy circle of chairs on the old spacious stage. Andrew had only recently reconverted the theatre back from the punk skate park it had been. "Underneath this stage," he said, "is the main bowl for the skaters!"

Awkwardly, Megan, Beth, Kazmega, Omar (aka: AOK), Andrew and myself sat looking at each other. Megan and Beth, friends, colleagues, and up-and-coming promoters soon made the introductions. I was introduced to Kaz and Omar, two local and notable hip-hop performers and promoters. I began explaining my concern with the 118 Ave. revitalization project—namely, whether it was created by the business elite to further exploit impoverished residents in Edmonton. Since I had only been in Edmonton for a few years—all of those spent at the university completing my PhD—I knew little of the community. It was my hope that these long-time and well-connected promoters could help me learn about the cultural community of 118 Ave.

For the next three hours Kaz and Omar explained the history of 118 Ave as well as the connections between *the Ave* and the local hip-hop scene. They explained that their major yearly festival *Hip Hop in the Park* had developed in this neighborhood and that this area continues to be an important center of local hip-hop culture. This festival, they explained, had been held yearly since 2008 on the third weekend of May to celebrate *Hip-Hop Appreciation Week*. This week was founded by KRS-One's *Temple of Hip-Hop* and "marks the anniversary of when Hip-Hop became an official culture sanctioned by the United Nations."[3] The Hip-hop Declaration of Peace encourages the recognition of hip-hop "kulture" as: an international culture of peace and prosperity. It is also a set of principles which advise all hiphoppas on how to sustain the peaceful character of Hip Hop Kulture and to form worldwide peace. Additionally this declaration is meant to show Hip-Hop as a positive phenomenon which has nothing in common with the negative image of Hip Hop as something that corrupts young people and encourages them to break the law.[4]

During the conversation with Kaz and Omar, it became clear to me that Hiphop Kulture was playing an important role in community development on the Ave. but the hiphoppas were, at the same time, engaged in an ongoing revitalization struggle themselves. While hip-hop could be used as a vehicle to aid in a community conscious revitalization of 118 Ave., the Hip Hop community was also struggling to articulate their own cultural revitalization. All of us felt that both revitalization projects could, and perhaps should, occur simultaneously. The question however is how to make this happen. What followed was a series of conversations with Kaz and Omar and a third participant, another key local hip-hop artist, college radio DJ, and educator, Marlon.

Together the four of us began to explore the struggle hip-hop musicians were having locally. Hip-hop had been introduced to Edmonton in the 1980s and, like many other places around the world, it flourished. It seemed that each time it flourished, the most notable participants, the mature artists around which younger artists, audiences, and fledgling industry gathered, left the city for a larger urban center. In very few cases, they returned.

To some extent, this was to be expected. The vibrancy of the hip-hop scene in Edmonton palled in comparison to other urban centers, such as Los Angeles and New York City. The changing dynamic of the hip-hop scene make us recognize that our discussions were predicated on looking at Hip Hop as a type of ecology. Artists, audiences, and industry were all interrelated and relied upon each other to develop. Howard Becker called this ecology an *artworld* (1982). The normal functioning of a music artworld produces a dense network of inter-relations which Christopher Small called *musicking* and describes as:

> Members of a certain social group at a particular point in its history are using sounds that have been brought into certain kinds of relationships with one another as the focus for a ceremony in which the values—which is to say, the concepts of what constitute right relationship—of that group are explored, affirmed, and celebrated. (1998, 183)

I wish to add Becker's *artword*, which focuses on production, to Small's musicking, which focuses on performance, to provide a larger view of the continuity between art and life that we call Hiphop Kulture. Hiphop Kulture is not an art piece upon which we can gaze at a safe distance and evaluate. Hiphop Kulture is a living cultural ecology within which we become enmeshed as we participate. This view of art is difficult to describe. The philosopher of environmental aesthetics Arnold Berleant argues: "Joining with continuity and engagement is the new dynamic character of art, shifting the deceptively static condition of art to a vital, almost disquietingly active role" (Berleant, 1992, p. 61). Recognizing cultural ecology requires a shift in perspective from art-as-an-object to art-as-culture-in-environment. And as in any ecology, health is based upon the health of the entire system. Viewing Edmonton hip-hop as an urban cultural ecology provides a frame to evaluate the fluxes and changes in the health of the ecology that the members have experienced.

The most recent flourishing occurred in the wake of Eminem's *8 Mile*. Kaz and Omar both got involved in hip-hop because of the film. They began looking for underground hip-hop battles. They soon found a few participants to take part in these types of cultural exchanges and helped to create many others. They realized that they were involved in creating the culture that they had been looking for. Their participation made them the hip-hoppers they wanted to become.

The hip-hop world has changed since the 2002 release of *8 Mile*. For instance, various technologies impact how hip-hop is produced and consumed, while large-scale business leaders continue to limit the expression of Hip Hop through their packaging of what they believe will spark consumers to buy hip-hop related products (e.g., CDs, videos, zines, concert tickets, clothing and other projects and services). I questioned whether hip-hop battles and community performances would resonate with youth who were new to the world of hip-hop or whether they would still appeal to people who were attracted to hip-hop by *8 Mile*.

I found that more and more Hip Hop intellectuals are increasingly staying at home making mix tapes and *YouTube* music videos. Kaz is fond of telling a story about a local would-have-been hiphoppa who developed some prominence following the release of one of these videos. This rapper was encouraged to finally perform live. Immediately following his first performance attempt, he walked off the stage, vomited, and never performed again. Kaz, Omar, and Marlon all agreed that most of the young people getting involved in hip-hop locally are staying at home and not getting involved in the culture of hip-hop. Or perhaps, they are looking at hip-hop as a product and not as a culture.

After some additional meetings, it became clear to us that both the 118 Ave and Edmonton's Hiphop Kulture were suffering from forms of cultural erosion. We reasoned that a healthy economy, community, and art practice all required a healthy community base. The question was however, what was the larger force causing the erosion? We guessed that perhaps the most obvious culprit, hinted at in the 7th Principle of the *Hip-hop Declaration of Peace*,[5] was neoliberalism.

NEOLIBERALISM AND CULTURAL EROSION

In a world increasingly reduced to budget lines, the social significance of the arts,[6] and its civic potentialities, are generally overlooked and undervalued. Financial reductionism is not new.[7] The transformation from political economy to economics in the late 19th century, and its recent cultural elevation, is only one indicator, although significant, of a larger process of the financialization of daily life.[8] More recently, neoliberalism has deepened this transformation.[9] Increasingly, public policy decisions are made on the basis of quantifiable data, efficiency, and profitability (Lacher, 2006, p. 153) while the "state and the arts had been transformed from a discourse on tastes and morality to one of economic rationalism and political collusion" (Kapferer, 2008, p. 3).

A survey of popular music textbooks supports the hypothesis of a growing acceptance of neoliberal evaluation of popular music. The discussion is limited to a history of successfully produced popular music products created by an industry for consumption. Music, in many cases, has been reduced to music as commodity. Popular music courses have become the canonization of the popular music industry. There is rarely a focus on courses that critically engage the students in the evaluation of the production of cultural music in a culture of cultural businesses.

Henry Giroux warns that, "in the society of consumers no one can become a subject without first turning into a commodity" (Giroux, 2009, p. 31). It is this subject, the very one that is produced for sale by the popular music industry, that targets young people to "deal with their lack of self-confidence, powerlessness, and the endless indignities heaped upon them in a consumer society" (59). Producing subjects for the popular music industry is big business. There are many specialists employed who are responsible for unearthing how to manufacture pop culture to young people. For instance, they provide ready-made songlists to over-worked instructors, who use this as solution to a problem. It certainly is much less complex than the "neuromarketing which uses magnetic resonance images (MRI) to map brain patterns and reveal how consumers respond to advertisements or products" (59). It is within this ecology of influence that much popular music appreciation is now nested.

TALKING COMMUNITY HIP HOP

Kaz, Omar, Marlon and myself, now with the awareness that we were confronting not just something peculiar to Edmonton but a much larger cultural shift towards neoliberalism, set out to develop a collaborative approach to research. Since, from our perspective, neoliberalism is a philosophy of individualism and extreme market freedom, our confrontation may begin with the opposite—a focus on community and a resistance to reducing our discussions to market value alone. From here, we began creating a larger circle of local hip-hop artists, presenters, and educators to share our experiences with neoliberalism. We realized that it was impossible to confront neoliberalism by generating one town hall meeting. We tried to address other issues, which were personal rather than systemic in nature, in this fashion on a few other occasions, but we found little success in this approach. If this was going to be effective to confront the dominant ideological force impacting our lives, we determined that we needed to build upon a methodological foundation.

LEARNING TOGETHER IN A CULTURE CIRCLE

Setting up the culture circle was very easy. I met again with Kaz, Omar, and Marlon and explained the idea of the circle very basically. They had, in the meantime, organized a facebook group and began to invite participants. Our Hiphop Kulture circle marked the first time hip-hop educators in Edmonton sat together and discussed their projects, approaches, and histories. Everyone in the room was a recognized leader in the Hip Hop community and was invited by another member of the group. The energy was very high as everyone introduced themselves and their projects. This was a new experience for everyone. Hip Hop musicians here, as elsewhere, are provided very little organized support from professional music organizations or local urban radio stations. The desire to "speak back" provoked many who gathered in our culture circle to share their experiences with neoliberalism and hip hop.

Freire, as reported by Dee Williams, began to teach literacy—not by teaching reading and writing first—by bringing community members together to "identify issues that impacted their daily lives" (Williams, 2009, p. 4). This approach to group discourse can "be used as a tool to problematize existing social relations and help move us towards a more democratic society. It creates a liberatory space where participants can questions the nature of social reality and construct their own" (11). By facilitating this culture circle, I hoped for two outcomes. First, I hoped that as a group we, as Hip Hop educators, would begin to discover our shared interests and responses to hip-hop's (neoliberal) public pedagogy that was eroding participation in local Hiphop Kulture. Second, I was hoping to find a dialogically oriented research methodology to revitalize the hip-hop community and the urban community.

CONSCIENTIZAÇÃO[10]: APPLICATION AND FINDINGS OF THE CULTURE CIRCLE

In Freire's *Education for Critical Consciousness* (1974/2010), he makes the distinction between naïve consciousness and critical consciousness. Naïve consciousness "simply apprehends facts and attributes them a superior power by which it is controlled and to which it must therefore submit...resigned to the impossibility of resisting the power of facts" (39). Critical consciousness, on the other hand, "is integrated with reality" (39). To be integrated into reality means to have a dialogical relationship with the production of reality. This stance towards reality puts the power to construct one's own reality directly within her or his power. The act of confronting reality will lead, Freire asserts, to the development of standoff between the way things are and the way they could be. It will subsequently lead to a standoff between the powers that construct reality in their image and the image of the world of the oppressed. The power of critical awareness emerges when the oppressed realize they have the power to change their reality. This awareness leads to the transformation of the oppressed into a conscious community willing to work together with a clear focus on what needs to be done to make their community better.

THE CULTURE CIRCLE: TOWARDS CRITICAL CONSCIOUSNESS

I was interested to see if the culture circle could be used in Edmonton's Hip Hop community. I was hoping that this strategy could be useful in our contemporary urban society, but I had no reason to believe that critical transformation would occur in this context. I was skeptical a critical conversation could invoke a project of humanization through a "conscious action to transform the world" (Freire, 2010, 81).

The Culture Circle as a Situation

It is, indeed, towards world transformation that Freire encourages. It is a humble revolution built upon very small steps. Freire presented each culture circle as a "situation." The goal was not to show people that they are not powerful, that would not be helpful at all. It would only add to the already oppressive feeling of powerlessness that is already engendered through public pedagogy. The "situations" at hand would become the social levers to aid in the development of the participants' conscientization, or the becoming of critical consciousness. Therefore, I believed our culture circle should begin with a "situation" with which we could all contribute. I decided to begin with a discussion about learning Hip Hop and how that has changed over the last few artistic generations.

The response to this opening situation led us into a conversation about Edmonton hip-hop specifically. Hip Hop artists in Edmonton have developed a community based dialogic and dialectical approach to hip-hop. This experience, like Freire's *pedagogy of the oppressed*, has developed from the confrontation local creative workers experience with the products of global music industries. Community based urban artists are people who have turned to art's expressive language out of necessity, and often to hip-hop by intuition and opportunity. Hip Hop was felt to be valuable as a language and expression because it celebrates individuality without the expense losing community. It does so by providing an approach to voice that is historically oppositional and emotionally potent. It is the intuition that Hiphop Kulture may provide a remedy to feelings of alienation central to the popular music industry. Titi, a spoken-word artist, summed it up as follows: "I didn't know what it was I was doing or even looking for. But the moment your intuition follows something and it collides with your experiences...you start your own poetry and use your own voice". Everyone in the circle could "resonate" with Titi characterization of their emergence as artists and educators.

Hip-hop in Edmonton is inseparable from both community development and global capital. The relationship between community Hip Hop and the mediated product of hip-hop is sophisticated and dialectical. The popular music industry produces cultural products that are widely circulated. Many of the men in the group, like Kaz and Omar had earlier shared, were "turned on" to hip-hop by *8 Mile*. The music industry, building upon already existent community art practices, takes and distributes hip-hop globally. Young people watch Eminem and recognized his alienation and the use of his talents as a way to rise up out of a violent world. They could "resonate" with this strategy and felt that they could use their talents to rise up out of their "situation".

However, some of these young people also view *8 Mile* as product meant to inculcate the masses to support the neoliberal agenda. They learned to separate the product of Eminem from the social message that makes *8 Mile* socially significant. Instead of buying into the Eminem liberation mythology by purchasing liberation oriented products—itself a trap of global capitalism—some chose to emulate the artist behind the product. This emerged as the first lesson of street pedagogy: *become an artist not a copy of a product.*

Kaz and Omar, who were both first turned onto hip-hop by Eminem, developed themselves as artists not as copies of a product. They began to work to emulate Eminem's battle style from the film while also looking for the underground battle scene. Kaz is fond of remembering that "In my first rap battle I took on this great big Cree rapper and made fun of his widow's peak...I thought he was going to kill me afterwards. We still laugh about that. And that's the day I met Omar (aka: AOK)". Real social networks were organized around what was learned from the movies.

Max, a cultural worker from a hip-hop education program called iHuman, said that: "We've all heard about the white kid in the suburb that gets turned onto hip-hop. Well that's me. I felt like I was on the outside looking in. I wanted to be inside that culture so I came looking for it. I didn't want to be outside anymore." Max identified with a vibrant urban culture on TV that he decided he wanted to join. He began looking downtown to find that community.

Awareness of "I am hip-hop, We are hip-hop"

Becoming aware of the social significance of an urban music community through the channels of public pedagogy sets the stage for contradiction. Public pedagogy, regardless of the lessons it purports to teach, functions within the framework of global capital. As illustrated above, public pedagogy teaches individualism and capitalist accumulation. But it also teaches speaking over listening because global media, until very recently, only went in one direction. This domination of medium over audience, and star over community, instructs youth about forms of human organization. Vertical organization, in the form of rigid hierarchy, becomes normalized where democratic organization, and horizontal networks, becomes rare.

Most people experience popular pedagogy as the pedagogy of domination. We are taught that "greed is good" and that our social role is to dominate and collect. But for many of us domination does not feel natural or good. In our alienation we recognize ourselves in the dominated. The apparatus of capital accumulation in popular culture have recognized this and have incorporate products for the dominated groups as well as the dominant social actors. *8 Mile* is just one example. In our culture circle we recognized that by emulating Tupac/Notorious/Eminem/Snoop, we have the potential to developed technical skills for hip-hop. However, our contention ran into serious contradiction. We recognized that is was improbable for us to move from the underground to above ground—to follow Tupac/Notorious/Eminem/Snoop into the spotlight in the hip-hop world. Therefore, we realized that emulating hip-hop leaders is not a fruitful ways to develop as artists. Our development must take place locally if we are to have healthy Hip Hop ecology.

For women, the contradiction is doubled because there are few artistic role models. Megan, a local MC and workshop facilitator said: "Rap is empowerment" but that she had to find her own way. She learned that "hip-hop doesn't tell you to stay in your clique it's about the medicine of hip-hop culture. It's about how to treat people". To achieve this aim, she had to overcome the sexism and male exceptionalism of hip-hop. Through this dialogue, the group realized that women must work with men to create a balanced cultural ecology, and men must work to help women MCs take their place in the culture.

Overcoming the mediated image of hip-hop learned from the channels of public pedagogy provided local hip-hop artists their first experience of *Conscientização*. This helped these artists identify a *product-oriented* vision of hip-hop culture and move to embrace a *life-oriented* hip-hop. Hiphop Kulture as community pedagogy became much more than learning the techniques of rapping; rather, it became thinking about life differently. Local hip-hop's community oriented pedagogy provided a dialogic approach to learning in community. This was the second lesson of our culture circle: *"I am hip-hop, I am my message, and hip-hop is my culture. We are hip-hop"*

LISTENING AND FLOWING RUBRICS

The third lesson extended our confrontation with public pedagogy. This lesson is built upon the first two (beyond the product, and we are hip-hop) and goes further to incorporate some directions for community Hip Hop pedagogy. There are six skills that the research team identified which must be part of a socially-generative Hip Hop pedagogy. In community pedagogy, these skills are often learned through a mix of trial-and-error and peer support. It is beyond the scope of this chapter to unpack these skills in any great detail or attempt an application to formal music pedagogy. Therefore, the remainder of this paper will provide a breakdown of how these *listening and flowing* skills are developed and how they work together in the production of local hip-hop.

Listening and *flowing* are the two parts of this community's Hip Hop pedagogical method. These two components, when fully developed, are experienced as a single competency. However, the development of most of these skills happens in partial isolation. For instance, each of these two main components can be broken down into three parts: formal, critical, and intuitive. In both cases, the level of abstraction moves from the least abstract (formal) to the most abstract (intuitive). Listening skills develop over time and through practice. *Formal listening* happens when

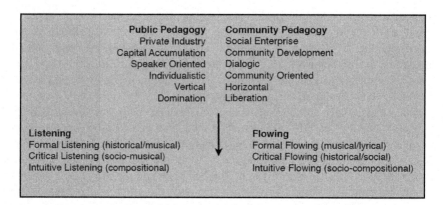

listening to albums and singles and is guided by community discussion. These discussions, the dialogic aspects of listening, help community members associate performers with styles and sonic textures. Much more research needs to be undertaken to understand this process.

Critical listening maps styles and sonic textures onto social discussions. The sound of Chuck D's delivery, for instance says, just as much as his rhymes. The development of critical listening is an extension of formal listening which often remains pre-verbal and intuitive. Through social convention, we come to understand and associate textural sounds with socio-political ideas and identities.

Developing a palette of these sound-meanings is a next step in the development of listening. This process is also dialogic and happens within style communities[11] and goes a long way to explain the connection between sound and politics. In the learning process, these associations are explicit. Errors are pointed out and mistakes or errors in judgment are often noticed and discussed. The division between novice and skilled performers is evident in how completely internalized the connections are between levels and how originally they can be demonstrated in their art. The demonstration stage I call *Intuitive listening*.

Intuitive listening is a compositional style of listening that is very active. It is a type of *reading of sound* that skilled listeners engage in. It is this process that makes it possible to have sophisticated listeners engage with sophisticated messages. Although I call this type of listening compositional, I do not mean to imply that only people who can compose music have this ability. In fact, before someone can begin to compose music, they must develop this type of listening. Only then can they move onto *flowing*.

In this community-oriented pedagogy, *flowing* represented the making of Hip Hop. Once the first two stages of listening have been developed, the first stage of flowing has already begun. *Formal flowing* happens when one is beginning to understand the building blocks of rhyme, rhythm and meter that are central to hip-hop. *Critical flowing*, the next step, happens in a much more abstract and temporal way. Critical flowing makes use of the socio-musical and historical-musical palette developed in the first two listening components and draws out, compositionally, sound and lyrical codes and presents them in new ways. Critical flowing is a level of complexity above formal flowing as it requires the composer to function at multiple dimensions at the same time.

The final stage of the community pedagogical process is *intuitive flowing*. As suggested in the word, intuitive, all of the other five tasks have been mastered and internalized, before the artist functions as a community elder and leader. I do not want to try to pin this skill down because it is very rich, complex and difficult. It is the most, and perhaps only, seemingly metaphysical aspect of the Hip Hop pedagogy. A number of culture circle members referred to it as "intuition" or to Hiphop Kulture as "the eternal creative spirit", or "the special human intelligence that you can't teach." It was generally agreed that the best art, including Hip Hop, is illustrating a distinct voice through the representation of life.

CONCLUSION: CREATING HEALTHY URBAN CULTURE ECOLOGIES

The first culture circle ended with the realization that in the next *situations* the community needs to address how they think about their larger culture. A great emphasis was been placed on becoming a good performer; however, there was little thought put into developing the audience and industry aspects of the culture. These are the remaining social ingredients needed to develop a healthy ecology. The culture circle provided the context for this community to recognize that Hip Hop pedagogy has been targeted primarily to "distressed" communities. Hip Hop education programs have been developed to help youth who are considered vulnerable because of their proximity to crime or because of their class or immigration status. Yet, little has been done to education youth generally. We realized collectively that much more work needs to be done to educate the general public about how Hip Hop propagates pro-social values and relationship as well as to dispel the mythologies of violence and misogyny that the mainstream music industry associated with urban youth and the hip-hop world. Further, we also need to engage in a larger discussion of the skills required of hip-hop performers *and* listeners. Too often the skills of listeners are overlooked and left underdeveloped. The impact of this omission is significant. Without developing listener skills an important aspect of the ecology is undermined. The popular media does a great job at listener education. Our circle has decided that it is time for us to do the same. This means that we will have to develop partnerships with local music educators to work out ways to help develop listener oriented Hip Hop education for the youth of our city.

Focusing on Hip Hop ecology provided a new framework to discuss the different yet equal roles that need to be played in order to have a healthy and productive ecology. In this way our culture circle in Edmonton remains to be very rich and though provoking. We are beginning to understand the complexity of social and economic revitalization.

Cultivating a cultural ecology is difficult work. It takes a great amount of time, dedication, and patience to develop the questions that need to be asked and the skills to answer them, once posed. We have also realized that we need to continue to develop diverse relationships within the circle itself. Not everyone is interested in developing a pedagogical program for the general public. Some participants are only interested in training new rappers. Some participants want to work with the local government to improve the conditions of the community, while others believe private initiatives have the power to eliminate the forces responsible for the oppression of most global youth at today's juncture.

All of these things need to be valued. We are realizing that there is no one solution to revitalizing our ecology, whether it is local hip-hop or a neighborhood. The solution is to develop a rich and complex cultural ecology that values egalitarian and community minded participation whatever that may look like. Perhaps, this is our first real lesson in community revitalization.

NOTES

[1] Originally published as "Hip-hop Citizens: Local Hip-Hop and the Production of Democratic Grassroots Change in Alberta". In *Hip-Hop(e): The Cultural Practice and Critical Pedagogy of International Hip-Hop*, Brad Porfilio and Michael J. Viola (Eds.), Peter Lang Publishing, New York, 2012, pp. 95–109. Reprinted with permission.

[2] Tin Pan Alley was the music-publishing center of New York City during the early 20th century. The name is now synonymous with the centralization of music industry practices and the music *product* that it famously developed. It changed the relationship that composers had with their craft and created a Fordist approach to music products.

[3] For more information please see Hip Hop in the Park *About.* Accessed: http://hip-hopinthepark.ca/home/about/ June 22, 2011.

[4] For more information please see The Hip-hop Declaration of Peace online at http://www.declaration-of-peace.com/en Accessed June 22, 2011.

[5] The 7th principle reads: "The essence of Hip-hop is beyond entertainment: The elements of Hip-hop Kulture may be traded for money, honor, power, respect, food, shelter, information and other resources; however, Hip-hop and its culture cannot be bought, nor is it for sale. It cannot be transferred or exchanged by or to anyone for any compensation at any time or at any place. Hip-hop is the priceless principle of our self-empowerment. Hip-hop is not a product."

[6] John Dewey in *Art as Experience* (1934) wrote: "The acknowledged community of form in different arts carries with it by implication a corresponding community of substance" (199).

[7] The erosion of liberal values is not new. Historians have noted the beginning of this process in the depression of the 1870s which "undermined or destroyed the foundations of mid-nineteenth-century liberalism which appeared to have been so firmly established" (Hobsbawm, 1975, p. 63).

[8] Randy Martin suggested that a turn towards financialization provides "Paths to action with definable results that clearly distinguish good from bad in measurable terms of success and failure" (Martin, 2002, p. 10).

[9] David Harvey has argued that the emergence of the neoliberal state tended to favor "strong individual private property rights, the rule of law, and the institutions of freely functioning markets and free trade. These are the institutional arrangements considered essential to guarantee individual freedoms" (Harvey, 2005, p. 64). Harvey's discussion of the history of neoliberalism suggests that free-market economics became synonymous with the freedom liberalism promised. It is, paradoxically, the freedom movements of the 1960s and 70s which set the stage for market driven decision-making as an expression of freedom itself. This type of freedom, for Harvey, is a regressive version that

has lost the social and civic underpinnings. Bill Dunn echoes this: "Individualism is at once the great achievement and great limitation of liberalism. In the name of freedom it provides an enduring challenge to totalitarianism, past and present... In positing freedom against collective oppression it denies the possibility or desirability of conscious, collective decision making" (Dunn, 2009, p. 13).

[10] In Paulo Freire's *Pedagogy of the Oppressed* he wrote that: "the conviction of the oppressed that they must fight for their liberation is not a gift bestowed by the revolutionary leadership, but the result of their own *conscientização*" (Freire, 1979/1993, 49). *Conscientização*, does not have a direct translation into English but has been variously translated as *critical consciousness* or *consciousness raising*, or *to become conscious*. Each of these translations refers to a process of developing a critical awareness of one's own dispossession by engaging in dialogue which focuses on the contradictions experienced in one's own life.

[11] A style community is a local group which shares aesthetic approaches. In a mediatized society, like ours, a style community may include members who they do not actually have any direct contact.

YEGH3[1]

(Edmonton Hiphop History) as Project-Based Learning

Hiphop Kulture and Hip Hop, the elements of its practice, are slowly democratizing Aesthetics and aesthetic education. The democratization of aesthetics is significant because it introduces a critical cultural dimension into aesthetics where none before existed. Aesthetics is still, for the most part, marked by universality that postcolonial scholars like Walter Mignolo (2011) identify as a hallmark of modernity. In the first part of this article, I will discuss the emergence of 'African-American aesthetics' (Caponi, 1999) or 'Black Aesthetics' (Neal, 2000) and these artists' critical consciousness resonating at the heart of Hiphop Kulture.

In the second part of the chapter I will introduce a pedagogical approach that has emerged from my work in Hiphop Kulture, engaged art pedagogy, and the project-based learning methods that I have begun to employ as a consequence. I have found that as an aesthetics educator responding to the democratization of aesthetics, project-based learning has become an important element of my higher education curriculum. I will introduce and discuss, with student feedback, one example of project-based learning, a microhistories iBook on Edmonton Hip Hop called YEGH3.

FROM HIP HOP CITIZENS TO HIP HOP HISTORY

This journey began with my 2012 publication, Hip-Hop Citizens, where I discuss the centrality of informal/community pedagogy in 'street' Hip Hop education. As a note, I have since taken up KRS-ONE's approach to writing Hiphop Kulture/Hip Hop/hip-hop from his 2009 Gospel of Hip Hop, so I would now have titled it Hip Hop Citizens. I have since been engaged in community dialogue with members of the Hiphop Kulture circle and Hip Hop citizens, or hiphoppas, featured in that publication. These conversations have strengthened my commitment to a critical pedagogy of aesthetics that, inspired by John Dewey's Art as Experience (1934), Maxine Greene (2001, 2004), and bell hooks (1990, 1994, 2010), might provide a basis for rethinking aesthetics education through Hiphop Kulture. But I am also less naive to the difficulties that must be faced in the development of engaged arts pedagogy. I have identified in particular, two aspects of this challenge. First, there is the struggle to stay true to the goals set out by Paulo Freire in Education for Critical Consciousness (2010) and Pedagogy of the Oppressed (1970), expanded by bell hooks as engaged pedagogy (hooks, 1994; Florence, 1998). The challenge is to develop an approach to Hip Hop education that emerges authentically, from Hiphop

Kulture. These are theoretical issues informed by community concern. More than one hiphoppa has expressed to me that school-based educators need to be sensitive to the cultural impact studio-based curriculum will have on Hiphop Kulture when the Hip Hop elements are reframed for classroom use. This is an area where music theory, cultural studies, and music education cross, and a rich direction for future research, that I refer to as the cultural studies of aesthetics education.

The second challenge, which might be called the public pedagogy of hip-hop (c.f Henry Giroux, 2009), stems from a lack of research on the cultural impact of global entertainment products that transform Hip Hop elements (usually rap and graffiti art) into commodities for sale as 'authentic' Hiphop Kulture. While there is a mountain of theoretical work by critical cultural theorists who discus this process, there are few community-based research projects that examine these speculations and provide social science feedback on the potential long-term cultural effects, although there is every reason to believe the impacts would be significant.

This situation might be complex enough if it was not for even newer struggles that Mark Anthony Neal frames as the post-soul aesthetic:

> In the post-soul aesthetic I am surmising that there is an aesthetic centre within contemporary black popular culture that at various moments considers issues like deindustrialization, desegregation, the corporate annexation of black popular expression, cybernization in the workforce, the globalization of finance and communication, the general commodification of black life and culture, and the proliferation of black "meta-identities," while continuously collapsing on modern concepts of blackness and reanimating "Premodern" (African?) concepts of blackness. I am also suggesting that this aesthetic ultimately renders many 'traditional' tropes of blackness dated and even meaningless; in its borrowing from black modern traditions, it is so consumed with its contemporary existential concerns that such traditions are not just called into question but obliterated. (Neal, 2002, 2–3)

Within this complex territory I am working towards the development of Hip Hop pedagogy. My approach began with Paulo Freire's Pedagogy for Critical Consciousness (2010) documented in Hip-Hop Citizens. I formed a culture-circle of hiphoppas, all recognized as important community members. Over a period of months we discussed the above challenges and worked towards articulating our core concerns, our priorities, and next steps. I have since realized that I stumbled into Participatory Action Research (Carr & Kemmis, 1986; Fine & Torre, 2008; Noffke & Somekh, 2009).

At the close of the first phase of the Hiphop PAR, what we now call Cipher5, we collectively decided that we needed to develop an Edmonton Hiphop Kulture curriculum and that this must begin with a documented history of Edmonton's Hip Hop practitioners. YEGH3, Edmonton (YEG) Hip Hop History (H3) took shape. I leaned heavily on Freire's assertion that "the starting point for organizing the program content of education or political action must be the present, existential, concrete situation, reflecting the aspirations of the people" (2010, 95). We decided it is necessary to frame the development of Hip Hop locally so that learners would recognize their place, and their lives, within and through community Hip Hop history. We may be a long way from New York City or Toronto but we do have Hiphop Kulture.

What is at stake here is the opportunity to write a community collective history and in the writing of it, to work towards empowerment. Freire's Pedagogy of the Oppressed suggests this role for educators, just as surely as Afrika Bambaata's Zulu Nation and KRS-ONE's Temple of Hip Hop does for hiphoppas. This comparison is not a surface accounting. KRS-ONE, in his lecture at Temple University, said that low self-esteem is created when a person's "well being is connected to something outside of themselves" this, he argues, is the beginning of poverty. Freire writes in Pedagogy of the Oppressed (1970) that: "the oppressed, having internalized the image of the oppressor and adopted his guidelines, are fearful of freedom" (47). These different voices coming from different times both identify that the pain of domination will be overcome with the development of critical awareness and the expansion of imagination.

What I began to puzzle over in Hip-hop Citizens was how a critical pedagogy of Hiphop Kulture might be understood also as a critical pedagogy of aesthetics. But what I did not account for in that discussion was how the power of dominator culture is located in aesthetics. For instance, in the 18th century Alexander Baumgarten defined aesthetics as the science of how things are cognized by means of the senses but soon after, in 1790, Immanuel Kant redefined aesthetics as disinterested perception. Kant's definition has exerted a far greater impact on the philosophy of art in the Western tradition than Baumgarten's. Once disinterested perception became the basis for aesthetics, and not a scientific study of human expressiveness and meaning-making (a cultural study), only European Fine Art is included in Aesthetics. John Dewey's Art as Experience (1934) attempted to overcome Kant's mentalist construction of Aesthetics and more recently, both Terry Eagleton and Luc Ferry have pointed out that Aesthetics is really about an Enlightenment conception of individual/personal development and bourgeoisie morality (Guyer, 2005, 30) and little about an inquiry into human practices of expression and reception. Walter Mignolo (2011) has argued that the very notion of Art, upon which Kant's Aesthetics is based, is itself a social construction, used as a tool to establish hierarchies of expression that allowed European bourgeois cultural expression to dominate the rest with terms like folklore, craft, popular culture etc. Mignolo calls this technique the colonial difference.

In this chapter I contribute to this developing discussion by illustrating the way Hiphop Kulture challenges the colonial difference. And since the practice of Hiphop Kulture is found in the elements of Hip Hop, a class project that documents the local history of its practitioners allows for a foregrounding of a postcolonial challenge to Aesthetics, provides an opportunity for students to gain critical insights into the writing of history, first hand experience in doing the cultural studies of aesthetics, and has led to the production of a freely available educational product that will likely make a positive contribution to our community.

HIPHOP KULTURE IS ENGAGED ARTS PEDAGOGY

I believed for some time that I was applying critical pedagogy to hip-hop. But as I read more postcolonial theory, studied the history of aesthetics, listened more to hiphoppas, and watched my students coming into awareness of their place and responsibility in university and their city, I realized that I was missing perhaps the most important aspect of my project. Hiphop Kulture is critical pedagogy. I understand critical pedagogy to be an educational philosophy interested in developing socially oriented, critical consciousness that emerges when students are provided educational situations that engage with core values of democracy and social justice. The hiphoppas I worked with were all engaged in the development of critical consciousness, something central to Hiphop Kulture.

When asked about media messages of the culture he grew up on, in a 2004 lecture at Temple University, KRS-ONE remarked that the dominant theme was "everything that you have has no value". He goes on to explain that dominator culture works to convince you that your culture is valueless, and that the only way to become valued, to get validated, is to buy into its commodities, practices, and institutions. But there is a catch he says. These same institutions, the only ones that have the power to validate you, have created frameworks that keep you out. This negates any possibility of attaining the validation that you are told is essential. This is an impossible situation.

Gregory Bateson (1972) calls this impossible situation a double bind (271–278). He explains that it is technique of domination without the outward appearance of it, and sometimes, without the dominators even realizing they are upholding a system of domination. It works when a social actor, as a functionary of a system, makes two contradictory demands. This strategy is powerful as there is no way to solve the dilemma of the double bind within the system. If you stay inside the system you will forever remain trapped in its double pincers. While Bateson did not theorize the double bind with aesthetics in mind it is evident in KRS-ONE's story.

KRS-ONE explains that Hip Hop was a movement to "create an entirely different community". It needs to be noted that what emerges is a community based on aesthetics, Hiphop Kulture is a new type of community culture that is not based, necessarily on traditional notions of ethnicity, language, and geography. In this sense Hiphop Kulture is the emergence of a postcolonial culture based on aesthetics. This move is perhaps more complex than might at first be noted. It is not just that a group of people that were kept out of the dominant system created an alternative. It is more significant than that. The emergence and success of Hiphop Kutlure as an alternative aesthetic illustrated that aesthetics are cultural. Since this is so, then the philosophical discourse of aesthetics is also cultural and is the cultural product of European Art culture. The entire history of aesthetics is no longer a philosophical discussion of Art (universal), it is the detailed elaboration of one cultural system, one among a great body of other cultural systems, that is aesthetic systems, that are found all over the world. Art is one way of thinking about human creativity.

This realization, that aesthetics is a cultural system, also means that Kant's definition of aesthetics as disinterested perception only holds true only within the cultural system from which it emerged, and that we must reorient the study of aesthetics, so that it now might be the study of culturally informed aesthetics systems.

As you have likely already noted, when aesthetics is shown to be an aesthetic system, then the educational projects that serve it are also culturally bound. It is no longer enough to talk about music education, my area, or art education generally, we must now begin to research and experiment with culturally bound approaches to art/aesthetics education. Music education might now be understood as Western Art Music education, Hip Hop education, Jazz education etc.

Returning to the issue at hand, the democratization of aesthetics and the double bind of the colonial difference is a struggle that was hard won (if indeed it has been won, of that I am not certain). It began to take shape in the Harlem Renaissance, was forwarded by the Black Arts Movement, and now flourishes in Hiphop Kulture. Perhaps the search for Hiphop Kultural education will start here.

THE BLACK ARTS MOVEMENT

Inspired by civil rights and Black Power discourses of the 1960s, the Black Arts Movement was radically opposed to any concept of the artist that "alienates him from his community" (Neal, 1968), and was "the period extending somewhat beyond the defining decade of 1964 (the year of Malcolm X's rupture with the Nation of Islam) to 1974 (the year of Baraka's renunciation of absolute black nationalism), during which the category of 'blackness' served as the dominant sign of African-American cultural activity (Benston, 2002, 3). Black Arts built on Alain Locke's 1925 publication The New Negro and upon the Harlem Renaissance which focused on 'Blackness'. Kimberly Benston (2004) observes:

Blackness…a term of multiple, often conflicting, implications which, taken together, signal black American's effort to articulate its own of possibility. At one moment, blackness may signify a reified essence posited at the end of a revolutionary 'meta-language' projecting the community toward 'something not included here'; at another moment, blackness may indicate a self-interpreting process which simultaneously 'makes and unmakes' black identity in the ceaseless flux of historical change. (3–4)

By encouraging African-American artists to seek inspiration from an ancestral heritage as well as from the ghetto community, Locke believed a unique art "would emerge" (Fine, 1971, 374). Black Arts joined with Black Power to form a political and cultural movement within ghetto communities: "The Black Art Movement artists are linked to Black separatist politics and Black Nationalism. The social political and economic conditions of the country during the 1960's gave birth to the latter group of young, militant artists, who, disdaining the traditions of Western art, seek to communicate with their brothers and sisters in the ghetto" (ibid.)

This was the emergence of a separatist aesthetics. Its success depended, not upon eventual inclusion into aesthetics, but instead, upon creating an alternative, what Gayatri Chakravorty Spivak (2012) has called, aesthetics 'from below'. Walter Mignolo in Local Histories/Global Designs (2000) emphasizes the historical significance of this struggle:

> In the sixteenth century, when European men and institutions began to populate the Americas, founding universities and establishing a system of knowledge, training Indians to paint churches and to legitimize artistic principles and practices that were connected with the symbolic in the control of authority and with the economic in the mutual complicity between economic wealth and the splendor of the arts. (Mignolo, 2011, 20)

The complex relationships between aesthetics and politics (Werner, 1994, 213–218) often called by Theodor Adorno (1977, 1984, 1991) and more recently Jacques Ranciere (2000, 2005, 2007, 2010) the politics of aesthetic/politics of aesthetics is usually reserved for white artists. But "as analysts from W.E.B. DuBois to Cornel West and bell hooks have continually asserted: in African and Afro-American life, culture is politics and politics is culture." (Werner, 1994, 213). This is not unique to any particular culture as Gena Dagel Caponi notes:

> Through cultural expressions such as dance, religion, music, and play, societies articulate and transmit the ideas, values, and beliefs that bind people together. Within the very body of the expression—the form of the music, the shape of the dance, the worship practices of the religion—are embedded cultural values. The structure of cultural expression—the cultural aesthetic—reflects and supports the ethics of the society, reinforces its values and philosophy…they emerge from a particular culture in a particular way, and they carry with them what musicologist Gary Tomlinson calls 'archaeological rules of formation,' which means their structure has evolved over time in relation to their social function." (1999, 7–8)

Democratizing aesthetics education requires the acknowledgement that cultural aesthetics, because of the colonial difference, do not meet as equals. Just as postcolonialism works to undue political inequalities so too should Aesthetics informed by postcolonialism. The first step of this, as I have noted above, is to problematize Aesthetics claim to universality, by recognizing cultural aesthetics. This is an act of aesthetic deconstruction that, in this case, might be understood as "African-derived American Culture (Caponi, 1999, 17–31) and should perhaps be seen not so much in terms of participants of one system rejecting another aesthetic system but more accurately as an emerging into consciousness of a new paradigm. This new paradigm is not anti-Aesthetics, but always cultural aesthetics that function as complex social systems which inform the consciousness and identities of participants and observers. The act of aesthetic deconstruction looks like aesthetic separatism, I think, because there is a political need to create public space for new art systems. An assertion of existence and therefore, independence, is made by the emergence of aesthetic systems that have been 'othered' (and dismissed like Black Aesthetics, African-American aesthetics among many, many others).

The separatist aesthetics of the Black Arts is instructive in this regard. Black Arts mentors supported young, mostly African-American artists to take inspiration from their home communities, to recognize their unique perspective, their unique imagination, and to use their arts to help rejuvenate their community culture. Often this would take the shape of "boldly patterned murals painted on the decaying walls of ghetto buildings" (Fine, 1971, 374), community theatre, or literature based on street art and inner city life, that emerged from place-based imagination. That it might be also beautiful is not the only characteristic of significance, the way it might be for Aesthetics. It is also significant to note that the Black Arts, as Hiphop would later, is a place-based articulation of creative intelligence and a fully flourishing imagination blended with craft, that does not require acceptance from (colonial) art institutions. In this regard Blues, Jazz, the Harlem Renaissance, Black Arts, Soul, Funk as well as Hiphop Kulture's emergence, are some examples of postcolonial aesthetic movements that contribute to the decolonization of the imagination. But I do not want to generalize too much, nor make too grand a claim. These are not examples of victories, but a history of public struggles in the realm of symbols, meanings, and social orders.

As the political elements of Black Power Movement were finding their aesthetic expression in Black Arts, they found new expression "in the aesthetics of Afro-American dramatists, poets, choreographers, musicians, and novelists" who were defining "the world in their own terms" (Neal, 1968, 39). These elements, championed by a Black inner-city Avant-Garde, posed a challenge to aesthetics, stripping it of any illusion that it could, any longer, claim universality:

In critical theory, Baraka was instrumental in the creation of what became the 'black aesthetic' of the 1970s, as well as the 'vernacularism' of the 1980s, demanding that African American literature and music be examine in the context of the culture that gave rise to it, with particular focus on the oral traditions of storytelling, sermonizing, and music of all sorts—sacred and secular. (Caponi, 1999, 21)

Linda Martin Alcoff (2007), reflecting on similar findings between Foucault and Mignolo, remarked on the difference between hegemony-seeking versus subjugated knowledges:

Subjugated or local knowledges always tend to do less violence to the local particulars and are also less likely to impose hierarchical structures of credibility based on universal claims about the proper procedures of justification that foreclose the contributions of may unconventional or lower-status knowers. (80)

Black Arts works to undue the aesthetics double bind and creates a new aesthetic order rooted in local expressive practices that leads to critical awareness and liberation. We might see this in the words of Baraka writing about Black Arts aesthetics in a language with which Paulo Freire and Augusto Boal (2006) would resonate:

> Our theatre will show victims so that their brothers in the audience will be better able to understand that they are the brothers of victims, and that they themselves are blood brothers. And what we show must cause the blood to rush, so that pre-revolutionary temperaments will be bathed in this blood, and it will cause their deepest souls to move, and they will find themselves tensed and clenched, even ready to die, at what the soul has been taught. We will scream and cry, murder, run through the streets in agony, if it means some soul will be moved, moved to actual life understanding of what the world is, and what it ought to be. (Baraka & Harris, 1991, 76)

Baraka's career-long interest in showing "what the world is" is echoed in the street logic of Hiphop Kulture, keepin' it real. Marvin Gladney (1995) characterized this heritage: "Black art has always been rooted in the anger felt by Afrikan-Americans, and Hiphop kulture has remained true to many of the convictions and aesthetic criteria that evolved out of the Black Arts Movement of the '60s, including calls for social relevance, originality, and a focused dedication to produce art that challenges American mainstream artistic expression...Public Enemy's Chuck D refers to Hiphop as the "CNN" of the Black community" (Gladney, 291) The Black Arts movement contributed to a political "movement poetics" (Smethurst, 2003, 268) that helped create a symbolic politicization of the Hiphop Kulture voice that, as Rachel Sullivan (2003) points out, has subjective impact, "African American rap fans are not arguing that rap leads them into social protest, they seem to be indicating that it offers a counter-dominant message that they use as an affirmation of their experience" (Sullivan, 616). It is precisely this self-affirmation that characterizes critical pedagogy and why I think the study of postcolonial aesthetics movements like Hiphop Kulture, particularly to understand the cultural pedagogy used in the system, as an important basis for developing a culturally informed approach to music education that I call engaged arts pedagogy.

FROM ENGAGED ART PEDAGOGY TO PROJECT-BASED LEARNING

Building upon Freire's work and her own feminist and antiracist work bell hooks (1990, 1994) has critiqued tradition educational practices by noting:

> (a) the metaphysical notion of knowledge as universal, neutral, and objective; (b) the authoritative, hierarchical, dominating, and privileged status of professors;

(c) the passive image of students as recipients of compartmentalized bits of knowledge, which limits student engagement in the learning process by not considering them as whole human beings with complex lives and experiences; (d) the traditional notion that the sole responsibility for classroom dynamics rests on teachers; and (e) the Western metaphysical denial of the dignity of passion and the subordination of human affectivity to the rationality. She also points out that the reification of official knowledge from the implications stated above reinforces White supremacist, patriarchal, and capitalist ideologies. (Florence, 1998, 77)

These observations are in keeping with the above characterization of the colonial difference that dismisses cultural approaches to knowledge. To counter this hooks advocates:

(a) re-conceptualization of the knowledge base; (b) relating of theory to practice to make education more relevant and meaningful, (c) empowerment of students to assume responsibility in conjunction with teachers, for creating a conducive learning environment; (d) encouragement of teachers' pedagogical emphasis on learner participation and engagement; and (e) understanding of teaching beyond "compartmentalized" schooling, a longer term involvement, development of critical consciousness, and teacher/student self-actualization. In sum, in addressing issues that impact students' day-to-day lives, engaged pedagogy 'restores to education and the classroom excitement about ideas and the will to learn' while simultaneously nurturing critical consciousness in students. (hooks, 1994, p. 12, *cited in* Florence, 1998, 78)

hooks calls this project engaged pedagogy. The idea of engagement is also found in arts pedagogy and was forwarded by critical aesthetic education pedagogue Maxine Greene:

Engagement—the opposite of malaise and not-caring—has been trivialized in current times, as simply affect (certainly not as important in education as cognition) or as motivation (a way to get students to study the things teachers think they should). Engagement, to Greene, involved not just happy involvement or a motivational trick, bur rather 'arousing persons to wideawakeness, to courageous and resistant life'. (Stinson, 1998, 224)

Maxine Greenes' definition of engagement is connected to consciousness and "recognizes the contextual and positioned nature of consciousness: 'Human consciousness...its always situated; and the situated person, inevitably engaged with others, reaches out and grasps the phenomena surrounding him/her from a particular vantage point and against a particular background consciousness'" (Greene, 1988, 21, *cited in* Henderson et al., 1998, 193). The process of engaged music education therefore satisfies the coming-into-consciousness of the Freirian critical pedagogy but does so in a way that it retains, and perhaps, elevates the body-in-community. Greene warns that if the aesthetic experience remains inside "aesthetic experience becomes pure escapism, a vacation from the cares of everyday life…aesthetic experience is not just a state of being in a feel-good place: "Consciousness… involved the capacity to pose questions to the world, to reflect on what is presented in experience" (Stinson, 1998, 225).

In an interest to create this type of engaged learning environment in a university cultural studies classroom I approached members of the Hiphop Kulture circle to discuss the possibility of producing a project that would connect hiphoppas and university students. I had recently been experimenting with iBook author and thought that an iBook of Edmonton's Hip Hop history would make a compelling project that would solve our problem of needing a history book. I pitched the idea to the Hiphop Kulture circle and gained support. The project came to be known as YEGH3 (Edmonton International Airport letters [YEG] plus Hip Hop History [H3]).

There were two issues that I needed to address. The first was a curriculum issue, how would I frame producing an iBook as a class activity? The second, was another practical issues, how would we put the book together, that is, how would we write the history in a way that remained true to the aesthetics lessons learned above? The answer to the first question was project-based learning, and to the second, microhistories.

COMMUNITY KNOWLEDGE: PROJECT-BASED LEARNING

Project-based learning (PBL) is an instructional method advanced by the Buck Institute for Education that has a five-point definition:

(a) "Projects are central, not peripheral to the curriculum"; (b) "projects are focused on questions or problems that 'drive' students to encounter (and struggle with) the central concepts and principals of the discipline"; (c) "projects involve students in a constructive investigation"; (d) "projects are student-driven to some significant degree"; and (e) "projects are realistic, not school-like" Collabouration is also included as a sixth criterion of PBL. (Thomas, 2000, 3–4)

PBL provided an environment where students and I, along with two hiphoppas who attended class as community representatives, could engage directly with the production of knowledge. PBL allowed me to put this critical conversation into action. Student groups were paired with a historically significant Edmonton Hip Hop artist, as decided by the Hiphop Kulture circle, and were tasked to write their stories for the iBook publication. Students would finish the class with a new sense of their city but also would have a writing credit in a digitally delivered free cultural history book of interest to the Hip Hop community and likely to general readers.

COMMUNITY KNOWLEDGE: MICROHISTORIES

It was decided early in the process that we would not write a single narrative history, but instead present individual histories of 16 artists. We found that there were so many different perspectives and versions of events in these stories that we could not privilege one over the other. This observation was supported by a discussion on writing postcolonial history, how we might learn from the Harlem Renaissance and the Black Arts Movements, as we write 'our' history. It was further expanded by a close reading of Linda Tuhiwai Smith's (2012) Decolonizing Methodologies with special attention to the chapter on Imperialism, History, Writing and Theory. From these class discussions students engaged with the writing of their individual pieces, what we began to call microhistories.

Microhistories is the recognition that history is constituted by a swarm of localized acts and negotiations that in their totality is recognized by its impact and effect as history. In the introduction to Small Worlds (2008) John Walton, James F. Brooks, and Christopher DeCorse argue that while microhistory "eludes formal definition" (4) the "link between micro and macro perspectives is not simply reduction or aggregation but rather qualitative and the source of new information" (6, quoted from Peltonen). Instead of framing microhistories in terms of master and metanarratives I follow Gilles Deleuze, Felix Guattari (1983, 1987), and Manual DeLanda's (2006) philosophy of multiplicity and scale that recognizes that knowledge and experience are produced by influences occurring at different scales. Producing microhistories therefore is the act of documenting history at a personal and metroscale, instead of a regional, national or global scale. The metroscale allows the researcher to resist the types of generalizations that make enlightenment modes of history so contentious to postcolonial scholars. Knowledge exists in geospatial nodes (Mignolo, 2011, 84) and microhistory is a way of constituting these nodes. Further to this, constructing nodes plays an important role in a postcolonial aesthetics because as Maida's (2011) has recognized project-based learning is a critical pedagogy that supports "a sense of 'knowing-in-action' that emerges from participating in practice-oriented learning experiences" (763). Doing microhistory is therefore a method for engaged arts pedagogy.

YEGH3: STUDENT RESPONSES

The value of PBL has to be evaluated on the quality of the learning experience not on the quality of the product that is produced. While there is still much to learn about assessing the pedagogical value of PBL I will contribute feedback provided by students on their experience with the project.

The purpose of PBL for me was to create an engaged learning environment that would help students gain critical consciousness. One student's response illustrated this:

> For me, project based learning was as much about the process as it was the final result. At first we were 3 kids emotionally shackled by the bonds of academia, then we were rather fractionated with different opinions and dissent (which sometimes wasn't taken lightly), eventually, however, we used all of our unique talents to form a piece with direction, insight, and, most importantly, a message. Unlike many other 'group' projects that I've participated in as a Political Science student, this project demanded collaboration. It's impossible to capture the human spirit by merely dividing up the introduction, body, and conclusion to each different member- a common practice in other disciplines. This project demanded in-depth collaboration, emotional investment, and a common direction. By it's end, I truly felt that we had achieved something and I take pride in what we produced.

Student comments that illustrated their focus on process over product was a surprise for me as I expected that students would be product based. It was a pleasant surprise to receive some comments that illustrated an awareness of the importance of process:

> This has been an amazing journey that has opened my eyes to another culture that I would not have experienced otherwise because of this course. Music has the power to teach and connect people that may not be connected otherwise. This type of leaning (community based group work) was not easy at first because you have a group of different people coming together with different backgrounds/ideas for a project, but I learned a lot from the others in my group. I definitely found that I personally learned more and was engaged more with this type of "hands-on" learning. I am grateful for this experience that showed me that research does not have to be boring.

YEGH3 provided an opportunity for classroom theoretical work to reach outside the walls of the university to engage students in the life of their community, as one student remarked:

> I very strongly think that this type of class is important to have more of at the university level and in classrooms more broadly as well. I feel that this type of project-based learning really forces students to interact with their community and helps to show students that they are capable of doing actual, immediate work that really matters to a particular group of people, as opposed to only doing it for a gpa, resulting too often in ambivalence. Project-based learning lends itself to more engaged and enthusiastic students and I know, for me at least, this has made a huge difference in my academic career and has in fact changed the path I will take in graduate studies – highly recommended.

But I have also learned that PBL does not happen without some significant challenges for some students. As a number of students remarked the process had many periods of struggle:

Project-based learning helps you to step outside of your comfort zone by engaging in group discussion and teamwork. By doing this, critical thinking becomes more focused and more worthwhile by engaging you in topics you would have never thought about before. It helps to remind you that everyone has diverse experiences and opinions and encourages a more open-minded, patient way of interacting with our world.

I also found that PBL presented challenges for me in helping student overcome a learned resistance to pedagogical experiments. As many students noted, PBL is not a norm in university classrooms which has the potential benefit of being new. But this benefit is a double edged sword. There is a threat that if the project does not go well then students might feel let down by the process, perhaps even used. While I did indeed have periods of concern I am happy to note that the project was a success and student felt that their time was well used. It is interesting to note, as these following students have, that resistance memories are still so present:

[student a] Since Project-based learning is not a norm in university classes, I was at first skeptical at how this will work, but as I attended the classes and did the work I realized that this is the best form of learning. Writing essays and exams just allows you to reiterate what you have learned and then you forget right away, but project-based learning allows you to take everything that you have learned and actually apply it and create something that you can say is mine. You actually have something that you have produced rather then just an essay or exam that you don't even see or think of again. This is the best form of learning, it allows for the real world to collide with the classroom.

[student b] Overall I thought that the project based learning course was a nice change of pace from my other classes and I look forward to participating in another project based learning class in the future. It allowed me to fully engage in the subject material and further explore something that truly interested me. I enjoyed working with our hip hop artist and learning about the history in our own city of Edmonton. I was hesitant about the group project portion but we all worked together nicely with the same end goal. I'm looking forward to seeing our creation come together!

[student c] This process was chaotic yet rewarding. There was no carved out path and no procedure for this project, but this allowed for a deeply honest and intimate portrayal of hip hop history in Edmonton.

[student d] I was at first a bit skeptical because I'm used to more structured courses. But once my group and I began it started to flow. And I also enjoyed that the course promoted outside class interaction especially being able to interview artists.

[student e] This class was my first experience with project-based learning and it was probably my most enjoyable class at University. It was definitely challenging at times, mainly because I was forced to step out of my comfort zone, but it was well worth it by the end.

CONCLUSIONS

The PBL process and the product, YEGH3, pushed all of us (students, myself, the Hiphop Kulture circle) deeper into the issues that will ultimately inform our Hip Hop curriculum. In this process we learned invaluable lessons that we would not have come up with had our discussions remained only theoretical, or only practical. Finding a blend of theory and practice helped me see the value of developing engaged arts pedagogy.

One of the obstacles that I have been struggling to overcome is the divide between the world of culture creation and the world of aesthetics education in academia. The history of the Harlem Renaissance, the Black Arts Movement and Hiphop Kulture has illustrated that civil rights, ultimately the expansion of democracy, impacts all parts of our society, even (and maybe specifically) arts education. As an arts educator I am committed to learning these lessons and finding an education environment that can nurture democratic learning, and contribute, in some small way, to a better world. I am relieved that after this difficult work a student will comment that a classroom "pushes you to develop the skills necessary to create an environment built out of a deep respect and responsibility for the community, your team, and your work" and that learning might "expand the way we see society and the cultures within it!". The history of the Black Aesthetic is not just a history of African American artists; it is a history of community resistance that may help all students see their role in making a more equal society. As one student commented: "This project helped me connect with artists and musicians in my area, understanding that our experience of Edmonton was that of a community. It's hard to feel like there is a place for the arts in this town. Because of YEGH3, I saw that there were other artists, struggling to build the same foundations".

NOTE

[1] Originally published as "A Pedagogy of Cultural Sustainability: YEGH3 (Edmonton hip-hop history) as a Decentralized Model for Hip-hop's Global Microhistories". In *See You at the Crossroads: Hip Hop Scholarship at the Intersections. Dialectical Harmony, Ethics, Aesthetics and Panoply of Voices*, Brad Porfilio, Debangshu Roychoudhury, and Lauren M. Gardner (Eds.), Sense Publishers, Rotterdam, 2014, pp. 29–44. Reprinted with permission.

YEGH3

Edmonton Hiphop Microhistories

In 2010 I became interested in a city of Edmonton project called 'Avenue Initiative Revitalization' that aimed to "re-energize" 118 avenue.[1] Particularly, on one aspect of the revitalization, to make 118 Ave an "arts hub". I began attending community visioning sessions and meetings with 'an ear' towards making a contribution to creative economy research with a case study on how policy makers and community members collectively work towards the visioning and creation of an urban "arts hub". At one of these meetings I sat with hip-hop artist, Kazmega. Kaz and I talked about my interests and he suggested organizing a meeting for me with a few other area hip-hop artists. A few weeks later we had put together what would become the first hip-hop culture circle[2] that I document in my article "hip-hop citizens" (MacDonald, 2012).[3]

Discussion quickly moved away from 118 Ave revitalization to the city's Hip Hop culture. The conversation was far ranging but of all of the issues, education topped the list. The concern centered on a perceived loss of the community education model that had been central to Edmonton's Hip Hop culture since the 1980s. Gone were the face-to-face lessons and mentorship that was fundamental to hip-hop's 'street pedagogy'. Instead, YouTube was becoming a main vehicle for education and dissemination. And while members of the circle recognized the value of technology for sharing products and performances (most wished they had it when they were learning) there was a general feeling that mediated education alone, without the social aspects of 'street pedagogy,' did not help to develop well rounded hip-hop citizens.

Related to this was a realization that around the culture circle there was a great deal of information about the development of hip-hop culture in Edmonton. Collectively, we decided that two things were necessary, that the history of Edmonton hip-hop needed to be documented and that secondly, a hip-hop pedagogy (how to teach) and companion curriculum (what to teach) needed to be developed.

But while the hip-hop citizens at the culture circles agreed in principle to these needs, the how's-and-what's were very much up in the air. The only thing that was agreed upon was that the hip-hop pedagogy needed to come from the culture not be imposed upon it. In short, I was challenged to critically interrogate school-based music education and to develop methodological tools to study 'street pedagogy' to learn how this works. This amounts to nothing less than working towards, what a musicologist might call the music theory of hip-hop. The result has been the opening steps of a project to rethink aesthetics education from a particular cultural perspective, hip-hop culture, to produce what Arnold Berleant (2002) has called cultural aesthetics.

CULTURAL AESTHETICS AND HIP HOP PEDAGOGY

In the opening to Gariyatri Spivak's 2012 Aesthetic Education in the Age of Globalization she urges aesthetic educators to do aesthetics 'from below', to undue the universalism inherent in Schiller's classical-aesthetics education. One might be tempted to call her suggestion, scaffolded by her long established writing in postcolonial theory, postcolonial aesthetics. But this would be a misreading of the work, I think, because Spivak does not provide a blueprint for postcolonial aesthetics. An absence of postcolonial aesthetic theory is not a mistake, it is meant to be instructive. What Spivak illustrates is that 'aesthetics-from-below' must not replace one aesthetics-system (classical/Western/Enlightenment Aesthetics) with another, even oppositional aesthetics (postcolonial aesthetics). This would amount to little more than a move to replace one universal system with another. Her proposition is much more radical. Instead of having one Aesthetics, Spivak suggests refocusing aesthetics education away from one system so that we might begin documenting existing aesthetic systems.

And there is much to do, and much at stake, as bell hooks noted in her 1990 article An Aesthetics of Blackness:

> Many underclass black people who do not know conventional academic theoretical language are thinking critically about aesthetics. The richness of their thoughts is rarely documented in books. Innovation African-American artists have rarely documented their process, their critical thinking on the subject of aesthetics. Accounts of the theories that inform their work are necessary and essential; hence my concern with opposing any standpoint that devalues this critical project. Certainly many of the revolutionary, visionary critical perspectives on music that were inherent to John Coltrane's oppositional aesthetics and his cultural production will never be shard because they were not fully documented. Such tragic loss retards the development of reflective work by African-Americans on aesthetics that is linked to enabling politics. We must not deny the way aesthetics serves as the foundation for emerging visions. It is, for some of us, critical space that inspires and encourages artistic endeavor. The ways we interpret that space and inhabit it differ. (1990, 112)

Spivak's idea for aesthetic education in the age of globalization hinges, I think, on what I would call cultural aesthetics, that is, aesthetics informed by postcolonial theory. This might be called aesthetics of the subaltern and would engage in the type of politics of aesthetics that Jacques Ranciere (2000, 2005, 2007, 2010) has recently written much about. This project, what I want to call cultural aesthetics would take the lead from Walter Mignolo's suggestion in Local Histories/Global Designs that all knowledge is geospatial and historicized. This move would replace a would-be universal Aesthetics of Schiller (and the enlightenment) with a heterogenous terrain, a quilt of equally valuable cultural aesthetics systems. Documenting located aesthetics knowledge and history in its place would work to undue the hierarchical power of colonial aesthetics that Walter Mignolo takes on in The Darker Side of Modernity. This approach would do what Spivak calls for, it would be an 'Aesthetics-from-below'. Our contribution is to take first steps towards the cultural aesthetics of Edmonton hip-hop.

YEGH3: EDMONTON HIP-HOP HISTORY

YEG are the Edmonton International Airport call letters and have become, over the last few years, the way people in the city write Edmonton. H3 refers to the three H's in hip-hop history. Tasked by the hip-hop culture circle Andre Hamilton, Marlon Wilson and I worked together in a private Facebook page to put together a table of contents for a hip-hop history project. Simultaneously, I proposed a course, Hip-Hop Culture, to be taught during the Fall 2012 semester in the Modern Languages and Cultural Studies department at the University of Alberta in Edmonton. I and 49 enrolled students were joined by Andre who came to class each week as a representative of the hip-hop community, on a journey to create YEGH3. In keeping with Freire's critical pedagogy, I applied a Project-based learning model, where the students worked in groups over the semester to produce oral histories that we called microhistories.

MICROHISTORIES

We began our project with the recognition that the history of hip-hop so far has been mostly a history of successful American artists, and that success has not necessary been understood from the perspective of artistic production but by market standards. We are not saying that to be corporately successful means an artist is not artistically significant, but we are saying that one does not necessarily mean the other. We recognize that at this time we are contributing alongside other groundbreaking projects to document independent hip-hop history emerging around the globe (this very volume for example). Our interest is not to deny the incredibly significant impact that hip-hop artists in the U.S. have had, and continue to have, on hip-hop culture. Instead, we want to contribute to this already well known history of hip-hop, a microhistorical element. We believe that current technology provides an alternative approach to writing cultural history and we intend to make just such a contribution.[4]

We see microhistory as an aspect of Hip-Hop culture, which has always been defined by its variety, its heterogeneousness (Chamberland, 2001). Microhistory is the recognition that history is constituted by a swarm of localized acts and negotiations which in their totality, at any scale, is recognized by its impact and effect as history. In the introduction to Small Worlds (2008) John Walton, James F. Brooks, and Christopher DeCorse argue that while microhistory "eludes formal definition" (4) that the "link between micro and macro perspectives is not simply reduction or aggregation but rather qualitative and the source of new information" (6, quoted from Peltonen). Instead of framing microhistory in terms of master and metanarratives we follow Gilles Deleuze, Felix Guattari (1983, 1987), and Manual DeLanda's (2006) philosophy of multiplicity and scale that recognizes that knowledge and experience are produced by influences occurring at all scales. Producing microhistory therefore is the documentary of history at a personal and metro-scale, instead of a regional, national or global scale. The metroscale allows the researcher to resist the types of generalizations that make enlightenment modes of history so contentious to postcolonial scholars. Knowledge exists in geospatial nodes (Mignolo, 2011, 84) and microhistory is a way of constituting these nodes.

YEGH3 MICROHISTORIES: THE BEGINNINGS OF EDMONTON HIP-HOP

Curt Black/Mark Giles/Don Joyce/Teddy Pemberton

Edmonton was bustling in the 1980s, despite an economic recession and slow population growth. West Edmonton Mall placed the city in the Guinness Book of World Records in 1981, Wayne Gretzky led the Oilers to their first Stanley Cup win in 1984, and the city hosted the Grey Cup that same year. Mayor Laurence Decore coined the slogan "City of Champions" in 1987 in response to a tornado that swept through the southern part of the city – an event that would soon be known as "Black Friday."

This was also the decade in which a great artistic community continued to bloom. Many of the city's current arts festivals were founded between 1980–1986, giving it the self-proclaimed title of "Festival City." Most importantly for us, it was during this time that hip-hop first emerged in Edmonton.

Teddy Pemberton, better known as T.E.D.D.Y, is most often credited with introducing the sweet sounds of hip-hop to the city of Edmonton. Hailing from Brooklyn, steeped in early hip-hop culture, Teddy migrated to Edmonton sometime before 1980 (when exactly, we don't know). In 1980 he began broadcasting The New Black Sound Experience from the University of Alberta's campus radio station, CJSR. Pre-Teddy, hip-hop music in Edmonton was scarce, existing almost exclusively in the trading of tapes: the sale and exchange of rare, imported recordings. With The New Black Sound Experience, Teddy, as T.E.D.D.Y, had created a vehicle for hip-hop in Edmonton. From CJSR's Studio B, nestled in the basement of the University's Students' Union Building, Teddy blessed E-Town with hip-hop, reggae, funk, R&B, jazz, and the blues, musical forms entirely foreign to the synth-saturated airwaves of the early 1980s. Teddy's personal mantra was to play what he liked, says Roland Pemberton (Cadence Weapon), Teddy's son. Statistics from the Bureau of Broadcast Measurement indicate that Teddy's program was not only influential but popular. In 1998 his program garnered an audience of 1000 listeners per quarter hour; this is compared to a station-wide average of 300. Unfortunately, no earlier stats on Teddy's listenership are available.

Fellow CJSR DJ and Edmonton-based writer, Minister Faust, claims that Teddy was the first to refer to Edmonton as E-Town, a term that these days is nothing less than omnipresent in any Edmontonian's vernacular.

In 2010 Teddy was inducted into the Stylus DJ Awards Hall of Fame, an honour given annually to great Canadian DJs. Roland Pemberton accepted the award on his father's behalf.

B-Boy and DJ Mark Giles became interested in hip-hop in the early 1980s. Giles states that "at that time, nobody knew anything about hip-hop, it wasn't until breakdancing became popular that hip-hop culture started to get more exposure." The music "was still developing, every new song released brought some new artist to your attention who'd be trying to bring something different from the others." Hip-Hop was unfolding before his eyes and Mark was learning all he could from it. He would spend Saturday afternoons tuning into T.E.D.D.Y. on CJSR, and videotape breakdance crews on TV. With radio and television he had found his inspiration, growing into his own as a breakdancer and DJ.

Giles learnt to DJ by listening and practicing: "I learned to beat mix from local rollerskate DJs. All the scratching was learned from listening and copying, occasionally there may be a chance to see some on TV, a little later there were some movies but by then I had it figured out anyways." Mark also cited the movie Wildstyle as an important inspiration. Mark DJ'd at CKER, Edmonton's first multilingual radio station, as a friend of his hosted a show on Friday and Saturday nights. Sometimes he would hold hall and house parties where they would "kick it" and just have fun with the music and culture. He learnt about new music when people would return with fresh sounds after visits to New York. Sound connection, a now defunct record store, used to carry hip-hop; Mark recalls that they'd let you open anything and listen to it in the store. At this time, there was more of a focus on breakdancing than on DJing.

Mark fell in love with hip-hop culture as he found it to be a new and exciting means of self-expression. It was a movement, and while breakdancing died out in the late 80s to give more room to the music, Mark was clearly dedicated. His crew, "System 5" (active from 1984–85), competed at the Kinsmen Field House and the Jubilee, although it was more about the exposure and dancing than the competition. They would practice in their basements and at school, focusing mostly on ground work. Crews would meet up at Sportsworld, a roller disco on 104th street. Mark says "there were some really great breakers, though one name I remember is Curt Black, he was probably the tops locally."

Curt Black began dancing at age 12, in 1978. E-Town's own, The Hitmen, were an early influence on Curt's style, dancing several times on a local television program, Disco Days, between '77 and '79. The style was locking, what Curt described as a kind of full-body boogie. The scene was Sportsworld. Curt and his friends would ride the LRT to Coliseum station and walk the rest of the way to spend their Saturday nights grooving in a corner at Sportsworld. Their dancing, so far, was absent of the ground work that would later come to characterize the scene. The music video for Malcolm Mclaren's Buffalo Gals offered Curt his first exposure to breakdancing. Shortly after that came the music video for Gladys Pip and the Knight's, Save the Overtime for Me. Yet, very few possessed the means to capture televised performances, and so the kids, eager as they were, found themselves unable to dissect the technique of the breakers they saw on TV. That was until a friend of Curt's, one of the few with the means to record, captured Mr. Freeze, a member of New York's Rocksteady Crew, in action. Curt and his determined friends, Alastair Matthew, Ray Dean and Anthony were finally able to examine the formerly elusive institution of breaking. With a period of focussed training they were fast becoming competent breakers, the only breakers in Edmonton.

And so, with the skills only they possessed, Edmonton's first stumbled upon Legs, a downtown dance club and breakdancing's first platform in the city. The existing members of The Hitmen were hosting a dance contest there, and though Curt and his gang of friends were all underage, they were admitted inside to compete (standards have since become less lenient). They danced. And, as Curt put it, they "freaked 'em out". They buzzed and the next contest attracted many more dancers, eager to bear witness to the new style. After that, breakdancing got "bananas". Breakers flooded the streets. Sports World built a stage for dancers. Dance contests became bigger and more frequent. The first large contest took place at the U of A and drew a couple thousand spectators. A contest at the Kinsmen drew 5000. Groups from New York, Chicago and Toronto travelled to compete in Edmonton. Hip-Hop's various disciplines intermingled freely. Dancers Deejayed and DJs danced. Some dancers even rapped. Don Joyce, a friend of Curt's, did all three. They danced and spun whatever you could groove to, mostly hip-hop and early techno. Curt recalls that Herbie Hancock's Rockit and James Brown oldies: Superbad and Get on the Good Foot, were especially hot tracks. Following its explosion in the early 80s, breaking retreated into the underground somewhere around '86. Breaking had lived hard and died (mostly) young.

THE 80S HIP-HOP PIONEERS

DJ Dice

When you have a passion for something, it just sounds different. (DJ Dice)

Puma and Fila clothes were all he needed to look the part, but passion and eclectic beats are what set him apart. He can still remember how it began. It was 1983 when Chris Cousiño first heard Herbie Hancock's hit single "Rockit." In that moment, the fresh beats that had infected a generation ignited an obsession that would span decades; hip-hop took hold of his life. Hip-Hop was everything and it was made of everything: break dancing, graffiti, the look, and the swagger. Chilean by ethnicity, hip-hop came to take on an even greater meaning in the life of a student who felt alienated from his peers and his teachers. To the child who would one day become Edmonton's own DJ Dice, hip-hop would become his identity.

He was only four years of age when the violent coup d'etat of 1973 forced his parents to flee their homeland in search of peace. But even to this day, Cousiño feels a strong connection to his roots. It was an awareness of ethnicity and culture that preserved his identity among the other kids during the hard first years of his life in a new country. "I'm not like them," Cousiño says in the present tense—the distinction is clear in his mind.

As Chile defined his beginning, however, it was Edmonton that would come to determine his future. The Parkdale community of 1981, that the Cousiño family called home, was a melting pot of cultures. The rooms of McCauley School were filled with the children of immigrants—Italian, Portuguese, and a swathe of Spanish speakers. All these cultures became one in the classroom, in a way that Cousiño could not tolerate. He found salvation out in the hallways where a new type of education was forming: hip-hop. Where formal instruction failed to be relevant, hip-hop filled the gaps. For those that had no voice in the mainstream culture, hip-hop became their voice. First came the break-dancers, who exploded onto popular culture with the now legendary film "Beat Street." Then came the writers (graffiti) and the rappers, but all three were essential in the foundations of the tower of hip-hop—"There was not one without the others." The kids were taking cues from New York, but the power of original creation was in their hands.

Hearing the first record scratches in hip-hop beats, Cousiño became obsessed with learning these secretive DJ techniques. Originally a b-boy who travelled with his crew to other schools to challenge the best dancers, Cousiño took to the turntable and discovered a sleeping talent. He dove into any information he could get his hands on, many times relying on trial and error in an era where hip-hop knowledge in Edmonton was scarce and the highly guarded knowledge of an elite few. Dancers and other performers protected their styles from imitation and theft by confrontations that would sometimes erupt into full vendettas. It was in this viciously competitive atmosphere that Cousiño, now DJ Shadow to his peers, became recognized by other Edmonton talents like MC Point Blank, as being one of the first DJs to reach the same level of skill as the artists of New York. One by one, the young DJ had uncovered the secrets of mixing the best beats. Developing an experienced ear for the beat, he would soon be mixing in his own distinctive style.

You start scratching and you try any frickin' type of way of scratching—your elbow, whatever, anything—just to be different, just to show people 'I'm different.' It was something empowering that you had, that you could say: listen, I'm unique, you're nothing. That was our mentality.

Cousiño's style soon began to attract the attention of other aspiring DJs who attended every show to learn from the sidelines. Cousiño chuckles now, thinking of the mystified audience members who approached him after a recent set. He has grown from secretive miser of musical knowledge, into a willing sensei.

"They want to know how I did that, so I show them. Put your hand here. This is a scratch…"

In the beginning, however, DJ Shadow still had to prove himself. When he was approached by the sixteen year old Cousiño for a collabouration, MC A-Okay, a.k.a Bill Connelly, a rising star in the Canadian hip-hop scene, was unimpressed. In the MC's basement, DJ Shadow brought his equipment for a private audition and proved he could scratch with the best. After agreeing on a partnership, there was still one more issue on the table. Known for his love of taking risks, A-Okay had a daredevil attitude that he wanted to pass on.

"DJ Shadow, do you like to gamble? I'm gonna call you Dice."

The name struck a chord and become Cousiño's new moniker. Within six years, collabourating as "Simply Majestic," the duo collabourated with various Edmonton artists and released a full record that brought a major record deal. 1991's "We United 2 Do Dis" attracted national attention by winning a Juno Award, and built Edmonton's reputation as a center for hip-hop.

With the music and the dancing also came the look. B-boys were in constant pursuit of "looking hip-hop." Those lucky enough to vacation out east always came back from cities like New York or Toronto with items from exclusive hip-hop stores unfathomable to their friends. Those with connections made a business selling clothes and jewellery. The need to look hip-hop and set yourself apart from the crowd was so strong that Dice remembers spending five-hundred dollars on a tough looking leather jacket because "no motherfuckers had that jacket." The culture in all its forms, was empowering for those that took on its image.

But hip-hop culture included a dark side that was impossible to ignore. Dice acknowledges that "many of my friends growing up, they're dead [now]." This culture of gangs, drugs, guns and pimps "just seemed normal to [them]." It was common to go to someone's home and see guns lying on the kitchen table. He witnessed firsthand, the tragedy of some communities where the best hip-hop existed. Invited to stay with a relative in Chicago, Dice jumped at the opportunity to search for more hip-hop in 1992. Crossing a street in downtown Chicago, he suddenly found himself in the ghetto. The four and a half month stay made an impression that has lasted till this day – "I'm here. I'm in the urban jungle and everything's crooked and everything's bent." Tires burned in the street during the summer of a year where one hundred children died of gunfire, in front of beautiful graffiti murals.

Even despite warnings of danger, Dice went to the roughest areas to photograph because "they had the best graffiti." His obsession to learn and catalogue photos, records, and other remnants of culture has not faded in over two decades. Now forty-two, Dice confesses, "Even to this day, I'm addicted to...hip-hop." But it is not only an addiction to consume, but also one he hopes to share with those who are new to the culture. It's not about the money, and he has shown that through his volunteer work with Edmonton organizations like ihuman. Sometimes, people come up to DJ Dice after a set and he is amused by their amazement. Put your hand here. This is a scratch...

Andre Hamilton a.k.a Point Blank/Dedaliss

White walls, linyl floors, a record player next to book shelves brimming with books on metaphysics works by Jane Roberts and Michael Jackson's first moonwalk performance blaring on the TV.

In that moment, Andre Hamilton became was instantly transformed into b-boy and MC Point Blank. From a very young age, Andre Hamilton was immersed in music. His father was part of an internationally acclaimed group "The Rastafarians," and his mother, was a choir singer. Early on, Andre realized that performance was simply a part of his DNA. With close friend Bill Hallaway, he began pursuing his interest in hip-hop at Studio 84 in West Edmonton mall. Together they practiced cover songs as often as they could. This allowed them to transform their hobby into a craft.

New York City in the summer of 1987, when Andre was 14, he began to realize the impact hip-hop was having on him: "there were minor explosions, but 1987 was an atomic bomb of hip-hop and it spread globally like wild fire." During his stay, he met DJ Scott La Rock in a record store in South Bronx. The next year he spent all his time at school writing lines. All he could think about was hip-hop.

He started dubbing tapes with the help of his friend Steve, who also owned a set of turntables. Soon after he started getting calls for shows. Over the years, the many changes in Andre's stage names have mirrored the transformations he has undergone as an artist. For example, Andre's very first rap name was King. He describes the feeling of pride in his early raps when he first started performing hip-hop. It was a reflection of his African heritage. Everyone was a king. Later, he switched his name to Point Blank to create an element of danger. As time went on, he matured as an artist and a person and subsequently developed a disdain for the reference to violence that his stage name portrayed. During a period of self-exploration, Andre made an oath of non-violence. He chose a new name—Dedalyss—after the Greek god of flight. This name embodied his desire to move from darkness into light. It was in this moment that his spirituality was at the forefront of this life.

As Andre got older he realized that like many other art forms hip-hop feeds the soul but may not necessarily feed the body. So he went on to pursue post-secondary studies, while also working part time as a waiter. Ironically his main motivation to go to postsecondary was not actually a financial one but was hip-hop. He then received an opportunity from Much Music that allowed him to film a high budget music video with director Jordan Krizenowski. This is what sparked Andre's interest in filmmaking and explains why he chose to pursue a degree in film studies.

Andre believes with strong conviction that hip-hop is not simply a form of creative expression, but also a gift to oppressed and marginalized people. It provides hope and inspiration to the masses and facilitates stronger bonds within the community. He points out that the First Nations community has benefitted tremendously from this aspect of hip-hop. Their music, he says, is painfully honest and raw. Within it, you can make out the cries for freedom, and the cries for their ancestors. Andre mentions that when you hear an honest voice with real rage and real grief, you can't help but be affected by it. In this sense, hip-hop works not merely as a source of entertainment, but as a source of therapy. Hip-Hop has the power to heal a community, and revive a spirit of hope for the future.

Maximum Definitive

"I used to record everything and I would watch it and practice what I was seeing, to the point where I was no longer trying to be what I was seeing, I was just trying to be what it is"

The three members of The Maximum Definitive, David "Click" Cox, Justin Ryan aka "Darp Malone", and Roger "Mystic" Mooking each struggle to pin an exact moment where hip-hop came into their life. Like many it seems to strike an innate cord and once experienced, it was though it had always been there. From what would start as a large group of high school kids who battle rapped and b-boy battled at hall parties would turn into a trio whom would become one of the most prominent and acclaimed groups in Canada, placing Edmonton on the map and proving that a working class, industrial city can produce some great hip-hop.

It all goes back to the late 80's when Darp saw Click at a dance battle. It was the first battle Click, whom then went by "Style" and his partner "Finesse" had entered and they were intent to "blow peoples minds". They won the battle and created a name for themselves. The next day, Darp approached Click at Ross Shepard High School.

Darp had been battling and performing with his friend Jerome Louis and was in need of some backup dancers (they went on to add 2 more dancers, a DJ and even a female vocalist). In search of the perfect group name Darp grabbed a thesaurus and settled on The Maximum Definitive, which not only sounds cool but also creates a clean and memorable acronym. "TMD".

Roger "Mystic" Mooking eventually came to join the group during a pivotal time of evolution for TMD. TMD, of Darp and Jerome had done shows with Roger and his partner Shawn and the groups soon became friends. Disagreements between Shawn and Roger as well as Darp and Jerome resulted in Roger joining TMD and Jerome leaving. With Darps production and Mystics clever and intelligent lyricism, TMD gained its real focus and started to make a name for themselves. Soon they began traveling western Canada and opening for artists likes of Ice-T and The Fresh Prince. Slowly the group dwindled leaving only Click, Mystic and Darp.

Jordan Kryzanoswski approached the group after a performance at a fashion show and told them that he was interested in shooting a music video. They would go on to shoot videos for a couple of their tracks but the video that changed their lives was for the song "Jungle Man". During a different fashion show Much Music VJ and hip-hop gatekeeper, Master T showed a particular interest in both the group and the song Jungle Man which convinced the group to make a video for the song to submit to the Much Music Video Fact. Citing the X-Clan and Brand Nubian as key influences, the Jungle Man is a melodic slice of afro-centric hip-hop characteristic of the early 90's. The Muttart Conservatory proved to be the perfect place to shoot the tribal themed video.

Once the video hit the airwaves, the group gained nationwide attention resulting in a Juno nomination and winning the Much Music Video award for best rap video in 1993. The group was all still under twenty and Click was still in high school struggling to make the right business decisions in this sudden flood of success. Following the awards, Mystic decides to stay in Toronto since he had little to return to in Edmonton. While all three members knew they had to be in Toronto to really make it big, Click still had to finish school and Darp had a job and a girlfriend in Edmonton so they returned with plans of completing an album. It was during this absence where Roger naturally forged ties with fellow Canadian group Bass is Base whom he had met while on tour with TMD in Vancouver. This relationship built Darp recalls a key event in what would come of the group, "While im working and mixing the album I hear that Bass is Base is going to be performing on much music and hosting soul in the city or something. I remember sitting down with the family and I see Roger performing with them. And he wasn't in the group to my knowledge. They then showed a picture of the album and Roger was on the front cover. There was never a conversation between roger and I about him moving on and doing stuff with Bass is Base. I found out when all of Canada found out." This event essentially marked the ending of TMD. Unable to come to an agreement, production for the album ceased.

Though TMD split in 1994, it was not the end of their involvement in the hip-hop community. Click returned to Edmonton and had a radio show with Minister Faust on CJSR until 1994. He also mentioned Earl Henry aka E.Dot who is originally from Edmonton, played a crucial role in his and Darp's life by producing music with him. Mystic eventually went on to become a well known chef who is now the host of Every Day Exotic which airs on the food network and is also coming out with an album with in the next year. Click latter on worked for major record companies he says "from 2000–2008/2009. I worked for B&G and I worked for Universal music. I have been heavily involved with music all my life. Now I manage artists." Darp took on a career in I.T and has a family.

Task Force

> We were anti-system and organized society... screw all the hypocrites, screw
> the system, screw the government, fuck the police, like that... fuck it, in your
> face task force, preachers of wisdom. (Simon (Kilo) Ferguson)

Simon Ferguson and Shawn MacKay sounded nostalgic about their rebellious
and radical days in Task Force. Task Force, or Task Force Preachers of Wisdom
(P.O.W), was an Edmonton based hip-hop group in the early 1990s. In 1993,
they changed their name to Lions From Tha Den, and performed their final show
together as a group under that name. Their style consisted of rap, reggae, and rock
influences that collided to create a powerful and revolutionary political sound.
Shawn, or D.V.L. (Devil), got together with Roger from Maximum Definitive
prior to 1990 and started the group, but nothing became of it and they went their
separate ways. In 1990, Shawn discovered Diane McKay, or Lady Deshay, who
grew up singing in a church choir; after much persuasion, he convinced her to join
his rap group Task Force. Simon was recruited into Task Force around 1991–1992
to record a verse in the song "Raise Your Fist," which would later be the song
used for their groundbreaking music video. A local DJ, DJ Black Magic (Patrick
Pocorello) frequently helped Task Force perform at live shows. English (Wayne
Walker) became a member of the group in 1993 for a very brief amount of time
before the group dissolved.

The Edmonton and international hip-hop scene was a battle between mainstream
and underground in the early 1990s. "We had the mentality that our rap was still
underground, we're the hardcore rappers...we don't want to be a sellout and stuff
and do commercialized bullshit." At that time, recording CD's and producing
merchandise to sell to fans would cost more than $20,000. Because of this ludicrous
expense, Task Force never recorded a full length studio album: "We had short tapes
and songs half done but we didn't have a project pressed and ready to go at the shows,
maybe just some promo, demo CD's, but we didn't really have a product, and we
didn't really care either, it was just for fun. Get your music out there...and enjoying
it with your friends, that's what it's about for me." They did, however, receive a
VideoFact grant, becoming the second Edmonton hip-hop group to have a music
video on MuchMusic. The video for "Raise Your Fist" was a huge leap forward for
the group, getting their foot in the industry's door, and it made them more popular
than they'd ever imagined. September 11, 1992 was the day the group shot their
political and radical video (an almost eerie foreshadowing of the tragic event that
would occur 9 years later). After the video was released in October of that year,
people were calling them asking for their CD, and they had opportunities to start
touring, but none of them had been prepared for the popularity. "We didn't know it
would blow up, we were just doing it for the love at the time." When asked what set
them apart from other hip-hop groups in Edmonton, Diane said "We were the only

one that had a girl singer. And also Shawn was white, and Simon had dreads…we were different. That was really drawing to people. And we were radical."

Task Force, or by that time, Lions From Tha Den, played their last show in October of 1993. They never officially broke up as a group, there were "no hardship and no fighting, we just went our own ways." Their unexpected success was the biggest culprit of their dissolution. Had they been at different stages of their lives, I have no doubt they would have been one of Edmonton's most successful hip-hop groups. A reunion is not out of question, however, so perhaps Task Force will rise again as Preachers of Wisdom in the near future.

THE NEW SCHOOL

War Party

War Party is the most successful Aboriginal rap group in Canada. War Party is the first Aboriginal hip-hop act to have a music video in heavy rotation on national television. War Party is a movement that built a following from the grassroots up, starting with the reserve. War Party is just… real.

Take one look at Cynthia Smallboy, currently residing in North Battleford, Saskatchewan however, and you probably wouldn't believe it and neither did she.

"He forced me in," chuckled Cynthia, recalling her first performance with War Party back in 1995. Rex Smallboy, father and senior of War Party approached Cynthia the night before a scheduled show at the Maskipeton Cultural College. One of the original members of War Party (Bannock) pulled out last minute, and Rex needed a replacement MC. And quick. "I'm a poet," Cynthia insisted. "It doesn't necessarily mean that I'm a rapper." But Rex didn't care. With a single night of preparation (along with being profusely bugged by Rex till midnight), Cynthia at last agreed. "Okay, I told him," replied Cynthia, finally convinced. "I'll grab my baggiest clothes and… and see what happens."

With no prior experience and a couple of hours rehearsal, Cynthia didn't know what to expect, how to feel and how to react to being on stage as an Aboriginal female rapper for the very first time. She wanted to make that very clear to the audience as well. "K, I've never done this ever," were the first nervous words out of Cynthia's mouth: "I did my first performance without even wanting… without even trying to be a rapper."

Little did Cynthia know at the time that joining Rex on stage that night was one of the defining moments in War Party's history. A history that embarked and progressed down a road uplifting the voice of aboriginal youth to the mainstream media via hip-hop music.

Progressing to that point however, wasn't easy: "Most of the old people looked at our music as a bad thing," recounted a frustrated Rex. "They could hear the bad things: the "F this and F that. The bitches, and the money," so they wrote us off before they even considered us". The negative stereotypes of rap music had infiltrated the mainstream by the 90's, polluting the perception of the influential and instrumental, yet controversial musical cultural phenomenon of hip-hop for the reserves of Hobbema: "They were like, "you guys think that you guys are good role model for our children?" Clearly, "they" weren't paying attention to War Party's lyrics and Rex's message: "They started scrutinizing what we were doing and that got me mad as hell. I was nobody and yet I was putting myself out there for my people... and then what my people did? They attack us." Rex knew it was time for a change.

"We decided that we were going out there to change people's opinions. Tell people what it really felt like coming up as a Native Person in some Native community and the pain and the challenges of being a Native person."

These pains and challenges of life in Hobbema were all too well documented. With just over 15,000 people, the community of Hobbema has a per capita murder rate four times greater than Edmonton (The Edmonton Sun, 2011). In the 1950s oil was found on Samson Cree Nation land and in 1971 it was decided that each member of the band would receive monthly royalty cheques. As a result, drugs and alcohol became a hot commodity and gang turf wars plagued the four First Nation bands of Hobbema—Ermineskine Cree Nation, Samson Cree Nation, Montana and Louis Bull Tribe. With a dangerously high violence and crime rate in such a small area, RCMP officers have always secured a watchful eye on Hobbema, its community and more importantly, the youth.

"We were having problems with the police," Rex recalled, remembering his younger years. "NWA and "F*** the Police" really resonated with me and the whole teenage angst thing." This was around the same time as the Oka Crisis, the infamous land dispute between the Canadian Government and First Nations people in 1990: "I really related to the NWA song and I felt like Public Enemy really related to so much of what they were saying and what they were going through with social justice, discrimination and racism." A fiery, young Rex Smallboy was now motivated and determined: "I thought that if that guy (Chuck D) can do that for his people, I want to do this for my people... "When rap came along it transcended. It was so open you could make songs about anything: about love, about hate and about hurt... I wanted to create that... It was cool to be black...I wanted to make it cool to be Native."

It was crucial for War Party to define who they were and where they came from: "We didn't want them (the public) to misunderstand who we were and where we were coming from," explained Rex when asked about the origins of the name War Party. "I thought, K, well those old racist Hollywood movies where they have the Indians that come and chase the stage coach and a lot of time they say, "Oh, there's a war party coming..." so we thought okay, if we say War Party, they'll know that we were talking about us." It was really the music that gave them props though.

"My girlfriend at the time Cynthia had an amazing memory," referring to why Rex asked her in the first place. "Eventually I talked her into it and from then on she stole the show." There was an absence of well-known female Native rappers at that time, but once Cynthia combined her poetic background, astounding memory along with an overwhelming endorsement from Rex, she quickly overcame her shyness and became what Rex called, "a natural": "She started writing her own lyrics and she was amazing, a big part of what we did." For Cynthia Smallboy, it was all about owning the music.

"This was mine. This was my vice." Hip-Hop was a way for Cynthia to release tensions and to get her ideas out. "I was so in love with the idea of sharing who we were, as hip-hop artists with the people that would share who they were as a community."

Within the community was a teenage Karmen Omeosoo: "My nephew Ryan told me, "Yo I heard this kid he's about 13 years old and he sounds amazing, you have to hear this kid." Intrigued, Rex told Ryan to invite "this kid" over and if he was good, maybe they would consider throwing him in a track. After one session, Rex would go one step further: "He (Ryan) brings him over and he (Karmen) was good… really good. If there was anyone who really had that street sound, who was totally associated with rap, it was Karmen. With his passion for the music he really took on that persona."

With the core members Rex, Cynthia and Karmen (aka HellNBack) together, War Party's most stable (and well-known) lineup had finally been assembled. This lineup would release four full-length albums, three of which were nominated for the "Canadian Aboriginal Music Award for Best Rap or Hip-Hop Album", winning twice (in 2001 and 2002). Amongst War Party's catalog, their first single "Feelin' Reserved" strongly encapsulates the societal hardships that aboriginal youth face in growing up on reserves. The song's chorus:

Feelin' reserved, man that's how I'm living/I gotta do with this mic I was given/To try to get by, no word of a lie / We gotta try to restore pride.

There are two play on words employed in the chorus.

First: 'reserve' references both Aboriginal reserves and how they hinder (or "reserve") the development and opportunities for Aboriginal youth and second: by the pronunciation of "mic" sounding similar to the word "life", the chorus displays the sense of despair that Aboriginal youth on reserves feel in regards to the opportunities they have open to them and portrays hip-hop music (the "mic") as a means of escaping this reality. Furthermore, the statement of "try to restore pride" is a recurring theme throughout the song. Despite the struggles Aboriginal youth face, there is pride to be restored as it once was: "I remember the first time I saw "Feelin Reserved" on Much Music." said Rex, looking back. "got scared because of how our people are so judgmental. I thought "oh shit man people are gonna be mad at me for saying what I said."

At first, the Elders offered no guidance or support for War Party's movement. They were very hesitant to support the music and culture, merely assuming rap was all about "the swearing and the crotch grabbing on stage… We always think negative first… It's like we've been conditioned to believe that way," explained Rex, shaking his head, "I had to go in there and educate people and tell them, "look we're trying to help you guys make some changes we are trying to do something good."

After receiving coverage and praise from popular mainstream national television outlets, such as CBC and Much Music, the Elders and community of Hobbema finally started to clue in. They finally had an opportunity to see what War Party was actually doing: "It took a while for them (the Elders) to understand what I was trying to do was a good thing." But even then, they still had their concerns. The Elders told Rex and the rest of War Party, "Now you have to watch what you're saying and watch what you're doing because these young people are watching you."

With their rise in popularity, recognition and success, those young people watching were tuning in to the inspirational rap troupe from Hobbema perform on the national and international stage. Touring all over Canada and performing in Washington D.C. and even Japan. "Rap music is a beautiful thing. It's like a universal language," proclaimed Rex, reminiscing about War Party's time at the World Expo in Japan. "There was some Japanese cats that started rocking some freestyle... I didn't know what the hell they were saying but I can see and feel what they were trying to feel: Rap."

Despite the language barriers between War Party and the Japanese, the ability to relate and communicate while rocking some freestyle created a connection that Rex felt was truly magnificent and beautiful.

Cynthia, while appreciating the opportunity to visit and perform in Japan, felt a much stronger connection to her surroundings and environment while at the grand opening of an Aboriginal exhibit at the Smithsonian Museum in Washington D.C. "It was overwhelming." Being around so many of "her people" gave Cynthia Smallboy a breathtaking experience. "There was probably like 80, 000 Native people there. It was ridiculous." There were so many in attendance who were so much alike, yet so different and diverse. To avoid being lumped together, Cynthia made it clear to the audience and group: "Always make sure to tell people it's important where we're from." For Cynthia, it was Red Pheasant, Saskatchewan. For HellNBack and Rex, it was Hobbema.

When it came to Hobbema, Rex's vision was all about changes: "Back home, one of my homies comes up to me and shows me his graduation ring and says, "You know what this is because of you... when you came to Montana reserve you did that workshop and it inspired me. I graduated because of you and some of the shit you said when you came out to my community." Humbled, Rex told him, "Nah man, that's you. You're the one who had to drag your ass out of bed every morning."

War Party held workshops of empowerment and addiction and suicide prevention year-round. While on tour or while back at home in Hobbema, his vision was always to promote wellness, sobriety and positive change in the community and the self. They invited youth to visit, practice and record at their hand-built studio and facilities. They encouraged the youth to dedicate their music and lives to the commitment to make a difference in the community while sharing their own voice for change.

After a performance and workshop in Bearskin Lake a youth, still in elementary, told Rex, "'When I grow up I wanna be just like you'… that meant everything to me." Patting him on the back Rex told the young boy, "You know what? Just make sure to make a difference in your community when you get old." The reception and appraise for War Party went beyond the music as well: "After a show people would come up to us and say, "we don't even like rap music, but I liked what you said and what you did there." That really moved me. "

Rex added "I'm just trying to be a good leader in my own life and my own little family community… I'm just trying to make a difference. We have that responsibility," responded Rex when asked about his place in the community. "We have to try and lift up hip-hop music and rap music culture to get back to the fundamentals of where it came from, which was change."

But while Rex saw change happening in other parts of the world with his and the group's music, Hobbema was still crime and despair ridden: "I would be on the other side of Canada doing songs about suicide prevention and hear about people in my community committing suicide." The day that Rex graduated from a suicide-prevention course, one of his friends in Hobbema tragically committed suicide. Rex was upset that other communities were fighting to make a difference, but back home in Hobbema, he would see "nothing changed."

Frustrated, Rex and the group began to go through creative differences regarding song and business concepts. Looking for guidance, Rex asked the Creator to show him what he needed to be humbled. War Party would fall apart soon thereafter.

Today, Cynthia lives in North Battleford, Saskatchewan with her and Rex's son. Rex is currently in Vancouver, British Columbia and Karmen stayed behind in Hobbema, only recently relocating to Winnipeg, Manitoba.

Despite being dispersed throughout the country and no longer operating as a single unit, Cynthia remains proud of what they've done: "It's still part of who I am," said Cynthia, when asked about her life post-War Party. "I always make sure to make the time to respond to fans… There were lots of up and downs for us, and at the time we were so hungry for it… We wanted that real hip-hop feel," when reflecting on her time with the group, "We made it happen for ourselves."

HellNBack meanwhile would go on to launch the highly successful Team Rezofficial, winning the Canadian Aboriginal Music Award for Best Rap/Hip-Hop Album in 2004 for their debut album, "The Foundation". Their single "Lonely" (2009) would peak at the top of Much Music's RapCity charts.

Rex, although far west in Vancouver, still maintains his status as a resident of Hobbema, and remains determined to make a difference in his community despite being thousands of miles away: "When people ask me where I'm from, I always tell them that I'm from Hobbema," Rex proudly declared. "I've never been ashamed of where I'm from." Rex's message and stance towards change itself has never faltered. "I have a new single coming out soon, its called 'I Got Heart'."

Currently in the process of finishing the music video, it is due for release in early 2013. "I Got Heart" still embodies Rex's message of making a difference, a call for change and being a role model: "People don't allow me to forget my place with the music. Still today… it's almost been 10 years since we broke up and people still recognize me and tell me, "You inspired me to be a rapper," and, "You're the pioneer of Native rap in Canada." I don't look at myself that way… if I did, It would be all of us as a group that held it together…I'm just grateful because it all started just as a dream. I never thought that anyone would take this shit seriously."

Rellik

"For me it was Raising Hell by Run DMC" says Rellik. That was the moment he knew he was an MC. "After that I had to have fuckin' everything… KRS-One, Kool Moe Dee, LL Cool J, and DJ Jazzy Jeff & The Fresh Prince, just everything that came out." This obsession led Rellik to begin to write raps at the age of 13. He bought pawnshop turntables and a mini drum machine, started DJing, and eventually upgraded to a mini sampler. Rellik's skills as a producer and a performer were nurtured at Victoria Composite High School. As part of the school's music program, he learned about the equipment involved in music production, as well as how to write music.

Rellik's verses did not contain much in the way of socially conscious material when he first started MCing. He describes his first verses as more being about talking shit and battle rapping than anything else. He developed his rhymes by "just watching guys do it, then writing verses in [his] basement." It was in his first group, RIP (Redmen in Progress), which he and his group members began including social messages in their verses, which were mostly about native consciousness and oppression. While in RIP, the group toured throughout an "aboriginal circuit," which involved going out to various reservations and performing for the people. The next stage of Rellik's career was where MCing really took off for him. Rellik joined the group Victims of Society, where Shawn McKay from Task Force gave the group their first big gig, opening for Dream Warriors. After bouncing around with a couple groups, Rellik found himself producing a radio show with his future Won-18 group-mates on campus radio CJSR at the age of 16.

At CJSR, a close friend of Rellik, Billy Blackout, was in charge of the hip-hop segment of a radio program called "The All Night Dance Party." The show ran from midnight until six in the morning and featured an hour of techno music, an hour of house and then the remainder was hip-hop, R&B, and reggae, which Billy Blackout hosted. The chief engineer at the station, Ray Semenoff, had a "soft-spot" for the budding artists and let them use the studio adjacent to the radio show to record tracks in. Now, instead of recording tracks in his basement, Rellik and his friends had a studio where they record that had an 8-track reel to reel, a booth, a nice mic, and a board. Ray taught Rellik the basics of the studio while Billy Blackout was doing the show, and during their time slot at CJSR, Rellik recorded tracks, often bringing other friends with him. During the show, there was an opportunity for listeners to call in and rap live on air. This is how future Won-18 member, Plex, came to be the third future member of Won-18. "Plex's first rhyme came over the phone to CJSR on the show" reminiscences Rellik. After Plex's first on-air verse, he started coming into the booth at CJSR with Rellik and Billy Blackout. It was over the years during the radio show that Billy Blackout, Plex, and Rellik developed a relationship that would eventually lead to the formation of Won-18.

After leaving CJSR, Rellik and Plex opened The Dungeon, which at the time was the only commercial hip-hop specific studio in Edmonton. Rellik fondly refers to this period as the "Dungeon days". Having this studio was an asset to Plex and Rellik "as they had the keys," and could therefore come and go at their own leisure, also giving them their pick of studio times. This was not the case five years earlier when Rellik was still attending Victoria High School. Money was tight and primetime studio slots were expensive. Corey Johnson, who according to Rellik "should get more recognition in Edmonton hip-hop," ran the Southside Am Tek studios. He provided Rellik and Plex with cheap studio rates. The caveat being, they were scheduled from when the last session ended through to the start of the next session the following morning. Rellik and any friends who needed something recorded, would bus across the river and go straight into the studio. Meals, sleep and showers were missed, but the opportunity to continue producing music was not. Corey Johnson's amicable studio agreement with the future Won-18 members was later emulated by Rellik and Plex. A young Marlon Wilson, who would go on to be part of Politic Live, had a similar arrangement.

In 1999, shortly after the closing of The Dungeon, Won-18 released their first album titled 'Return to Edlantis. The title was a play on word of Atlantis, the lost city, for the reason that they saw Edmonton as the lost city for hip-hop in Canada. Return to Edlantis was initially released on cassette, "if that tells you how old we are" laughs Rellik, as he explains that the album was made a time before they had the technology to burn CDs. On the album was a random assortment of tracks, some containing a collabouration of all the Won-18 members, and other's solo artist tracks.

During the height of the Won-18 days, the group opened up for major acts such as the likes of Casual, the Hieroglyphics, and even Rellik's childhood inspiration Run DMC in 2001. Rellik recounts this proud moment in his career, while at the same time dating himself and how long he has been active in the Edmonton hip-hop scene. "Whenever I drop that name, everyone is like 'holy shit those guys must be old guys'...Jam Master Jay was still alive when we opened up for those guys. We've been doing this for a long fucking time."

It was a few years between the release of Won-18's debut album, and their second titled Dirty Boulevard. Rellik explains that in between the two albums, some of the group members started having kids, and Won-18 was put on the backburner while life took precedence. Dirty Boulevard finally dropped in 2005 but it wasn't without difficulty. All of the songs for the album were ready to go, but money was an issue, and Won-18 had to secure an investor before the CD could be released. Dirty Boulevard is a reference to 118 avenue in Edmonton, which is also how the group got its name. 118 avenue is an essential area of Edmonton to Rellik and the members of Won-18, as Rellik grew up in Cromdale and Plex in Beverly, it was the road that connected the two neighborhoods, and according to Rellik it was "here [that] it all happened." On the album cover of Dirty Boulevard is the Cromdale Hotel and Drake Hotel, two places that Rellik considered as monumental locations along 118 avenue.

Shortly after Dirty Boulevard was released, Plex moved to Toronto to further pursue a career in the entertainment industry and Won-18 became a loose collection of individuals, no longer a group. Plex came out with a solo album first entitled Brainstorm. Rellik signed with Plex's independent record label New Leaf Entertainment and started his own project entitled Mighty Mouth, which was released in 2010. Initially the project was financed and produced by Plex, however due to lack of resources, the duo experienced a business breakup. They were best friends, however, but Plex 'bit off a bit more than he could chew'. Luckily, Rellik was able to team up with Edmonton producer Fatty Jones to finish Mighty Mouth and distribute it.

Reflecting upon the success of Mighty Mouth, Rellik considers it to have done better than he expected. In mid 2011, Rellik considered the album to be dead in the water "it didn't sell a whole lot, but fuck nobody's CDs do anymore." In 2012, Rellik was nominated for two awards simultaneously, one was a Western Canadian Music Award for Aboriginal recording of the year and the other was a Aboriginal People's Choice Music Award for hip-hop album of the year. He was also invited to perform at the BreakOut West Festival in Regina. Although Rellik didn't win either award, he was flattered to be nominated amongst talent that he considers bigger than him and performed with them at the BreakOut West Festival.

One of the most important things Rellik shared was "All those years that we spent, we didn't know the fuckin business side of this industry, all we knew was beats and rhymes and doing shows." 'The music era has changed, and the only way you can sell CDs is by doing shows and touring now, you know? And that's the only way you can make your money is by doing that or getting radio play.' Had he known then what he knew now, Rellik feels Won-18 and his solo career would have gone a lot differently.

When asked about why he isn't involved in the production of mainstream songs destined for the radio, Rellik remarks that it would compromise his integrity and authenticity. "Hip-Hop will always be underground." By distributing CD's to small town music stores and gas stations, his goal is to spread underground hip-hop and hopefully break even in the process. It's not about the cars, chains, or selling drugs. "The only dope we slang is our dope music," Rellik said further commenting on his song 'The Dopeman' that was written in a similar metaphorical fashion as Ice T's "I'm Your Pusher." "Good hip-hop is out there, it just exists in a sea of mediocrity and you have to look a little harder to find it." This engagement with the ego, especially with young hip-hop artists is why Rellik believes Edmonton hip-hop is misdirected. "There are too many self proclaimed gangsters out there, claiming to be the number one rapper in Edmonton." Rellik acknowledges that he did come from a rough neighborhood where there was drugs and low income housing, but "it wasn't like it was Compton." He believes there isn't enough communication and no one is willing to work together. The North-South division that exists undermines the power of hip-hop to bring people together and instead builds barriers.

Errol Henry

It was 1984 and the hip-hop scene in Edmonton was repressed by emerging artists' lack of resources and insufficient knowledge of the music industry. Errol became a part of the Edmonton hip-hop culture with his friends Andre Hamilton and Chris Groove. They were taken under the wing of Mark Giles, the Godfather of hip-hop in Alberta. Together they learned how to make loops and sample tracks, ultimately discovering their love for the genre. They took funk and soul samples and put them through a 4-track cassette recording to create original beats that they could rhyme over. Young artists like Errol were limited to scheduled hip-hop nights at local clubs. As the hip-hop scene started developing, 182 emerged: a crew from the west end of Edmonton on 182 street. Every artist in the crew lived on that street from the neighborhoods of Laperle through Belmead; Aldergrove down to Callingwood. It seemed as though all of the talent came from that block. That is where the heart and soul of hip-hop music in Edmonton truly began. 182 street became the foundation for Edmonton's hip-hop scene and ultimately launched Errol's career.

He found his way out of Andre's basement, experimenting with sounds and hand mixing equipment to recording tracks in studios with his new crew. Together they opened for names such as Jazzy Jeff and the Fresh Prince, Ice T, Pharcyde, Maestro Fresh Wes, Dream Warriors, Michee Mee, Rascalz and Kid Capri. Errol eventually decided to change up the pace of creation and branch off on his own. He started calling himself Erl Da Ill Veteran which later evolved into Erldotcom. The Edmonton scene soon became too slow for Errol and he found himself unable to take his passion to the next level. Many artists become confrontational with one another and became more egotistical and self-centered. Errol described it as, "crabs in a bucket with everyone wanting to be the man." Eventually one of his good friends sat Errol down and told him the dream of being a rapper in Edmonton was unrealistic. Although this was very upsetting for the young artist, it sparked something inside of him that made him want to pursue this passion. He decided the best way to do that was to move to Brooklyn and become involved in a superior hip-hop community.

Moving to Brooklyn introduced Errol to an intense hip-hop community which helped him advance his career and begin to live his dream. He started making music with the help of Mr. Complex, a fellow hip-hop artist who produced his first vinyl record in Brooklyn. As his career developed and his name began to blow up, Errol was given the opportunities to tour in around North America and even play some shows in Europe including one in Berlin. Errol believes that Brooklyn and the contacts he met there played a key role in shaping his career into what it is today. He currently still lives Brooklyn and continues to work on new material as often as he can. "I started my new project before Take Me To Your Leader was even out." Some possible names he is thinking of are "boonoonoonoos," or "Where Do We Go From Here." Today Errol continues to rap for the love of the art and to express his many ideas and beliefs on life.

In today's hip-hop industry, it seems as though the actual music—the heart of hip-hop culture—has taken a backseat to the money and the fame. Up and coming artists all seem to be changing their style to get on the radio and to get on a label. Where it once was all about the creative process, now it is all about something that will sell. Errol is heavily influenced by early rap groups such as Public Enemy, fellow artists like Andre Hamilton and Darp Malone, but most of all, his family. His wife and kids provide a tremendous amount of support for Errol and everything he does, he does for them. Not only does he support them with his passion for hip-hop, but in his words, "I want my kids to know one day, that their dad was fresh and original." He believes that in order to make it in the current hip-hop industry, people need to be original, talk about real issues, and be their own individual. Some advice he has for young artists is to do it for the love and do everything with a meaningful purpose. Everything Errol learned while in Edmonton is still embedded in his music today.

EDMONTON TODAY

Touch

Nestled in the fields between townhouses that populated the Edmonton community of Belmead, Randy, long before he adopted the stage name Touch, and his former babysitter Andre were wearing the grass out learning to dance. They were learning the rhythm and moves that were the groundings in hip-hop, placing their hands upon the ground that would support the scene they were about to enter and help define. It was 1990 and they were over 3000 kilometers from Brooklyn. "If your city is not known for hip-hop, people just assume you can't do it," Randy says: "You could easily assume that hip-hop has to be done in a certain city."

Edmonton isn't a place that can be easily explained. If you're from here, it tends to mean something, if you aren't, well, you wouldn't get it. It's a city of average skyscrapers and sprawling housing developments. A city invariably wrapped in the past achievements of sports teams, banners faded; hopeful cheers of athletic glory a distant memory. "I grew up defending it, I'm a patriot of the city, through thick and thin. 1-8-2 (a reference to 182nd Street, where Touch and his colleagues in hip-hop grew up) became more hardcore, we called it that because it was a culture…Now I see cats with 1-8-2 tattoos and I think 'is that us?' We used to brag about how hardcore we were, being from there. But now it just is sketchy. It isn't something I brag about now."

"But the location and the city in general has had the biggest impact on my music. It's isolated, you don't know the scene…If we did shows out of town; we were disrespected. Because we weren't supposed to be good at it. I had a very antagonistic way of writing and dealing with that. Without the city I wouldn't sound or play the way I do."

In the early 1990s, Edmonton radio stations pushed back at the force of hip-hop. Stations like 630 CHED were filling dumpsters with hip-hop vinyl and promoting themselves with the phrase "No Rap Crap." Musical institutions in the Alberta Capital refused to listen to the music of hip-hop: the peoples' movement. And so, Edmonton's scene was forced to gestate underground, in a form that was raw, honest, and free from any major-label business restraints.

But the peer-to-peer networking aspect of the internet age has changed all that. "It's given people access," Randy says. "Which is good and bad. The blueprint of who to follow was narrow when I started, but with the internet there are rappers in every city, with every style, all with different goals. Back then your goal was to get signed, be famous, or be good."

It is of particular importance that Randy says be famous *or* be good. In the time without the quick connectivity of the cloud, being famous meant that you had to be sponsored. And with no pre-existing infrastructure for promoting hip-hop music in Edmonton, even talented artists had a difficult time breaking out into the public eye.

"I got Dre's (albums) in Denmark, three others in France. European countries get real hip-hop. They don't care where you're from, they just care if you're doing real hip-hop. They went through the same struggles as us. Where they aren't part of the scene, but it's the same thing. Hip-Hop was born in the USA but it didn't stay there."

As for the future of local hip-hop? "I want to see one dude that can eat off this city. One rapper that the whole city can get behind. You need appeal, but I don't know what else you need..." he concedes. Therein lies the tension of commerce and the Edmonton scene. No one made money, but the scene flourished without an established economy. However, in developing a removed microculture that did not fit the overarching societal framework of the city at the time, local hip-hop has ultimately faded from the collective memory of Edmontonians.

"I haven't changed my style, I'm comfortable with every decision I made. I drop an album every few years. I've improved, I work on things like storytelling but the fundamentals have not changed for me." Randy tells us, spoken like a man that knows his city and himself from lasting experience and struggle. "I just wanted to be good. As good as the people I was listening to just because I loved it. I wanted to listen to my stuff and be happy."

Politic Live

"The first time I ever saw anybody write a rhyme was in the back of a church, this girl named Debbie...the moment I saw [her] write that rhyme I knew I wanted to be a rapper. I went home...and wrote my own song called "straight out the ice age."

Growing up in sub-arctic Edmonton, with a strict mom, left little opportunity for Arlo Maverick of Politic Live to get into trouble. "If you're not into skiing or hockey…you're going to be stuck inside…the climate gives you a different perspective." explains Dirt Gritie, the self proclaimed hook man of the group.

Arlo Maverick adds "[That's why] we have some of the best djs…mcs… [and] producers, because… [the climate] forces us to be creative." Inspired by Debbie, Arlo began to occupy his time during Edmonton's notorious winters by perfecting his rap skills. Before long, he was pushing his cousins Dirt Gritie and Bigga Nolte to do the same.

Dirt Gritie explains: "When we were little little…Arlo used to write for the group."

Bigga adds laughing: "When I saw the love that Marlon got out of hip-hop, I decided hey, I want some of that too!" And with that, Politic Live was formed long before it officially existed.

The band has come a long way since their early days as the Immaculate Straightlaced Commarad playing high school pep rallies in the mid 90's. As the years passed, all three MCs developed their own distinctive styles. Arlo Maverick is the "de-facto leader", with a tenacity for social justice both on and off the mic. "Gritie is the ladies man…any Politic Live song that has to do with love was an idea that he started!" Arlo explains laughing, he adds, "with Bigga you're gonna get that charisma, that aggressiveness and rawness." DJ Sonny Grimez and Arlo met while working at an Athlete's world as teenagers. The two instantly connected over their mutual love of hip-hop, and Grimez helped to teach Arlo how to drive.

Grimez downplays his importance in the group: "My job is to save the rapper's breath" he grins. The group would eventually meet their "unofficial fifth member" Oozeela, who coincidentally turned out to be a distant cousin of Arlo, Gritie, and Bigga. Oozeela describes the working condition in the group as: "a family atmosphere…half on a mission, half just having fun".

The release of the group's sophomore album Adaptation catapulted Politic Live into the national eye, and changed everything, as Arlo says, "Adaptation put us into a different light, now we weren't just rappers from Edmonton. We were charting in the US, were getting played in Japan. So now it's like the city is expecting so much more out of you…"

Adaptation garnered widespread critical acclaim and numerous award nominations. The group remembers their first WCMA nomination as a highlight of Politic Live's decade long career. Arlo Maverick: "we were on top of the world… we all got dressed up…we got to a point where our music was being recognized by our peers."

"And the whole town [Moose Jaw] opened up to us!", adds Gritie.

With all of this recognition, why has Politic Live stayed in Edmonton, when so many others would have moved on to the larger hip-hop markets in Toronto and the U.S.? Arlo shrugs and responds, "Why would you not be a poet for your people… [and] represent your city?" Besides, "[it's] not just about Politic Live, it's about

Edmonton as a whole." This sentiment is loudly echoed in the band's most recent release, Ellipsis. From it's core Ellipsis is an Edmonton project, using entirely local producers, artists and photographers. Arlo explains: "of course we can work with producers from New York, but at the same time, if we want people to believe in us we have to believe in the people around us who are going through the same obstacles."

On Ellipsis, the song "Birth of a city" chronicles growing up in "Elympia", and illustrates the love/hate relationship most Edmontonians have with their city. Arlo says:

> With hip-hop its very much about representing your city…it shapes who you are. There is no one in this city that hasn't been affected by the boom and the bust. There is no one in this city that hasn't been affected by health care cuts… When these things affect you… [you] write a song about it.

Politic Live isn't only committed to staying in "Elympia", they're dedicated to using their success to create success for others in the community. They do this, not only through their exclusive employment of local artists on projects like Ellipsis, but also through Music for Mavericks – an independent music label that was started by the multi talented Arlo Maverick in 2002. Arlo views the label as a way of "keeping musicians employed."

As Ouzeela puts it, "universally a musician's life is difficult." Music for Mavericks provides a resource for local musicians to earn a living, without compromising their artistic integrity. The group also unofficially mentors local musicians. Arlo uses his experience in receiving government grants to help other musicians with the application process, and Dirt Gritie has mentored young Edmonton hip-hop groups such as TOA.

Despite the group's international success, and opening for countless hip-hop icons, when Arlo Maverick recalls the highlights of his career with Politic Live, the first thing that comes to mind is, "The first ever Hip-Hop for Hunger in Edmonton, I was like, we're onto something here." They certainly were onto something. In 2002 Politic Live organized Hip-Hop for Hunger, an annual fundraiser that has since raised a staggering 8000 + lbs of food for Edmonton's Food Bank. Arlo proudly adds: "Hip-Hop for Hunger was the first annual hip-hop event here in the city." The group's charitable contributions aren't limited to Hip-Hop for Hunger. Arlo also volunteers with The Keshotu Leadership Academy for youth, and Gritie hosts slam poetry seminars for inner city youth.

Through their critically acclaimed body of work, and immeasurable contributions to the city they grew up in, Politic Live has carved a permanent niche for themselves within the history of Edmonton hip-hop. The black t-shirt that Arlo Maverick has been known to sport aptly describes Politic Live's relationship with Edmonton: I AM YEG.

DJ Gamegirl

Sitting down for an interview at a Second Cup in west Edmonton we await the arrival of hip-hop artist DJ Gamegirl. We are admittedly a bit nervous and shy to meet the fierce woman behind DJ Gamegirl's intoxicating mixes. In the clubs she exudes a sexy confidence and a talent that has even the burliest of men paying their respects. While reflecting on this, at a small table near the entrance, in walks DJ Gamegirl. With a full smile she extends her hand and says, "Hi, I'm Priya." Priya looks demure and sweet. With her hair down and bangs pinned back, her look is a sharp contrast to the sexy outfits and wild hair she sports when she is working. She is however, no wallflower. Priya is wearing a grey sweater shirt that says in black writing, "I Love You Too, But…" She laughingly tells us, "if you notice, I love statement shirts. I wear them, obviously, all the time. I always have something to say. But, they are hard to find." After spending an hour and a half with her chatting, it is evident why such shirts are so appealing to her. DJ Gamegirl has a talent that is hard to find and wow, does she ever have a lot to say!

It was not until 2002, once her sons were older, that she took the risk and decided to dabble with DJing. She went to AXE Music on Wayne Gretzky Drive with a friend, who was also a DJ, to buy her first set of turntables. From there, she practiced DJing in her basement, unknown to anyone for nearly two years. She landed her first gig at a friend's comedy show in 2004, when in need of a DJ, Priya suggested to him, "well I can try." He was shocked that she even knew how, but gave her a chance. That night Priya set fire to the stage and ever since then her career has exploded. It was that evening that the man who later became her mentor, Love Jones, coined the name DJ Game for her. She wanted to be DJ Anonymous with the idea that she could play music behind a silk screen because of her stage fright, but Love Jones would not accept this. He knew her history and said, "girl you've got game". G.A.M.E is an acronym for "Girls About Making Ends." Priya is a fighter so she took on the name, which eventually morphed into DJ Gamegirl. From that night forward there has been no stopping her.

Her current success was a process and no easy feat. In the beginning everyone was encouraging of her aspirations, but when it came time to helping her, "no one wanted to give away their secrets," she reveals. She did all of the reading she could and confesses that she even bought a "how to DJ" book from Chapters. After highlighting, underlining and making notes, none of it really made sense because she is unable to read music. DJ Gamegirl has a natural ear for music that is not from formal training. She comes from a musical background, growing up playing instruments by ear and replicating people's movements. It was not until she gained experience DJing, that she was able to really understand the process and make sense of the book. She created mix tapes that she distributed to clubs as free promotion. Once her fourth mix tape dropped, people started asking her for them. She worked at many different urban locations and eventually climbed her way up the industry ladder. Priya has now reached a level of success that enables her to make a lucrative career for herself by picking and choosing her gigs.

She had to prove herself as a DJ, because being a woman she states, "they look at you like a joke." In an industry that has such a tight focus on sex appeal, often times she says she is hired for her looks, and they even tell her, "We don't care if you can play...you just look good behind the turn table." Her greatest gratification comes from shocking people with how good she is. As a woman she has to work extra hard to gain respect in a nightlife industry dominated by males. She tells us with the conviction that only someone with experience could have, "women are better DJs than men because they are more organized." Being organized allows her to create a flow with her music and be able to switch styles seamlessly to fit what the crowd is digging.

DJ Gamegirl's sounds have been nominated for numerous awards. This includes three Stylus Awards for "Female DJ of the Year" and "DJ of the Year in Western Canada." The latter she explains is more flattering because it is exclusive of gender identity. She sees herself as a DJ, "not a female DJ." DJ Gamegirl is all about empowering female DJs. She wishes that they could be seen on an equal level as men and she continues to strive towards that.

In Edmonton especially, there is a lack of female hip-hop artists. This fact alone pushes her harder to work for success. The Edmonton nightlife industry she explains, is monopolized. Being a woman they will try to take advantage of you. Often times nightlife business men will try and use her mix tapes for free, and say "it's good promotion for you. But, I've been promoting myself for eight years, I don't need that anymore, so I give them a price." It took a while for her to get herself to this position. Now that she has arrived here she believes things will only keep going up. Dreaming of one day opening for Nicki Minaj or Rihanna, these dreams may not be so far off. DJ Gamegirl has proven she is here to stay. We'll be listening to her until she decides on her terms that it's game over.

Titilope Sonuga

She steps up to the mic. Thoughts. Words. Sound. Reception. There is no second-guessing. No room for exceptions. She embodies all of it: the strength, the fear, the love, the hurt. She moves past it like nature running her course. Like a mantra she explains, "I am definitely closer to who I know myself to be because of my ability to exist in this art form." No hesitation in her voice, mind you, she didn't have that luxury.

7,937,932 people are packed into the lively port city of Lagos, Nigeria. She's winning the heat: second place in the race for the fastest-growing city in Africa, seventh on the list of fastest growing cities in the world. These are her roots. This is her home. At thirteen years old she's gone, thousands of miles away, tucked into the sparse suburb-city of Edmonton; population: 817,498.

This drastic change pushed Titilope Sonuga to define herself at a very young age. It strengthened the bond between her and her past, giving her something to cradle herself against and relate to. It was an instinctive interest in the art of oral traditions that inspired her in new directions. The fundamental expression could be the same, while the backdrop could be absorbed, re-interpreted, and re-focused. This convergence of her African roots and Canadian home allowed her to tap into limitless creative potential, leading her up to the mic in 2007.

Two years later the Breath In Poetry Collective (BIP) and Rouge Poetry was created with the help of Politic Live's Bert "Dirt Gritie" Richards and Ahmed "Knowmadic" Ali. Four years later, BIP and Rouge Poetry are still running strong, promoting spoken word in our city. You should stop by Rouge Lounge on a Tuesday night. It's a spot for the poets, the artists, the rappers, and the MC's.

And for the Edmonton hip-hop community, this sense of unity is integral. For those who believe spoken word poetry is meant to conquer and divide, guess again. A catalyst in the development of the BIP was the interaction between local hip-hop artists and the spoken word poets. Rouge Poetry works to facilitate and develop this relationship and network. When she started, it was through the hip-hop community that Titi found the support, mentorship, and encouragement she needed to develop her vision. She drew on the wealth of experience and knowledge from the hip-hop artists in our city to develop this collabourative venue. Rappers read their rhymes and then they bring the music back for their performances at the end of the night. In defining spoken word within the hip-hop community, Titi explains, "spoken word is a cousin of rap."

But what is spoken word?

It's sort of a rebellious form of poetry.

Without crutches. There's no pretenses, no highbrow elitism. You say something relevant, or you don't say anything at all. Simple. Social consciousness and artistic accountability is a fierce undercurrent in the work of a spoken word poet. Titi is no exception. Each poem she creates is crafted with the knowledge that she holds power in every breath. It's a responsibility negotiated by those who abuse it. And she doesn't back down from the weight of it.

You can see it in her "Brown Boys" poem. She shares a self-reflective perspective on this damaged, tortured thing that we have created and become completely enamored with. She articulates that as a society we have learned to feed on this destructive hate. Our own lives have become so fractured and disoriented that we create this media buffer to push against and protect us from our own flaws. It is one of the few illnesses we have failed to overcome. Which explains why history has repeated itself again. And again. And again...

This brings us back full circle to what we're doing and why we're here. Education. Our focus. Our aim. Paramount to our success or failure. She explains it all lies in our local community and talent. We have opportunity. We have promise. All we need is to harness it, and show our local talent a little more love. One of the primary obstacles? Keeping it here. Titi is adamant that as long as we keep looking to Jay-Z or Kanye, keep going outside of our local scene, we risk a little more of our own development and community. We need to move the art form forward by supporting our local artists. Starting Now.

NOTES

[1] Avenue Initiative Revitalization Homepage http://www.edmonton.ca/city_government/projects_redevelopment/avenue-initiative-revitalization.aspx (accessed November 12, 2012).

[2] The 'culture circle' is a technique I borrowed from Paulo Freire, the Brazilian critical pedagogue. The culture circle method developed out of Freire's need to create of form of literacy education that was community oriented. This requirement emerged from his observation that the 'non-literate' indigenous Brazilians that Freire was tasked to educate (provide literacy) were actively being colonized by the process of literacy education. But literacy education was necessary because industrialization was occurring and the only way to full participation was to have the skills necessary to engage with the system.

[3] I was interested in adapting the culture circle to ethnomusicology research because I found that during my previous research mine was the only critical voice and that to document an issue like revitalization required that I create and environment where I not only document direct effects but allow effected community members to critically evaluate the social, cultural, spatial, and economic impacts revitalization was having on them and their community.

[4] We propose to contribute a collected group of oral histories, the microhistories of Edmonton hip-hop, instead of writing one narrative of the development of hip-hop in edmonton (an enlightenment notion of history). We hope that YEGH3 might be a blueprint for hip-hop history so that in thirty years students will not be studying 'the' history of hip-hop culture, but will be able to choose amongst histories to explore the complex interconnections and interactions that humans weave in a media saturated world.

CIPHER5 AS METHOD FOR A CULTURAL STUDIES OF SENSIBILITY[1]

Aesthetic education, writes Gayatri Spivak (2012), is the preparation of imagination for epistemological work. I understand this as a potentially limitless archeology and genealogy (Foucault) of singularities (Rancière) formed at the crossroads of perception, signification, art technique, power (culture, institutions, politics), creativity/innovation, self, subject, and community. This very dense knot provides a one-sentence manifesto for arts educators willing to take up the epistemological and pedagogical challenges. And nowhere is this more necessary than in schools.

For complex historical reasons aesthetic engagement—engagement with sensuous knowledge—does not appear on most teaching and learning agendas. Critical Aesthetics pioneering educator Maxine Greene complained that: "I did not see this kind of passion in looking at young people from my adult vantage point. What I observed among adolescents was a pervasive sense of not-caring...I could find little enthusiasm for motivating students to engage in academic studies with little more relevance than the game of trivial pursuit." (1988, p. 25). Arts educators are not alone in this, but if we cannot get engagement in sensory knowledge figured out—in disciplines with aesthetics at the center—why should we expect success anywhere else?

Aesthetics experience is not limited to artistic practice, it is an important facet of general knowledge about the world as it has been in some schools of philosophy since ancient times. Epicurus, for instance, placed sensory experience at the center of his epistemology (Gordon, 2003; Klein, 2012). But as Foucault has pointed out, this lineage has been overshadowed by Platonic and idealist notions of aesthetics as concepts and ideas (2005). The sensory/empirical is almost always played down for the spiritual, or at least the metaphysical and, since Kant, Descarte and Bacon, in the name of Reason (Kincheloe, 2005). I wish to take another starting point, following the Epicurian line and place the study of, and teaching and learning in, sensory knowledge at the center of research of a critical pedagogy of aesthetics. This move returns aesthetics education to its ancient place as foundational knowledge, like literacy and numeracy, that gets transmitted by oral, aural, and visual sign systems and plays a core function in complex knowledge systems that include all registers of the human experience. As Greene notes: "Of course we need to introduce students to the symbol systems associated with the various arts, but we want to do so (or so I believe) to enhance their capacity to see, to hear, to read, and to imagine—not simply to conceptualize, or to join the great conversation going on over time." (Stinson,

1998, 227). Aesthetic education is distinct from the study of the history of specific arts practices and training in those expressive practices. It is "to help people to attend, to notice, to enter the particular state of consciousness that is aesthetic perception" (ibid., 224), to support the development of a rich and increasingly complex awareness of self. Aesthetic education is consciousness development of sensory experiences and the signification processes utilized to make sensory experiences meaningful.

But there is little space for students to engage in this type of learning. Aesthetic education is often reduced to Arts training and aesthetics equated with art appreciation (Blumenfeld-Jones, 2012, 42; MacDonald, 2013). Most alarming is that the consciousness that Greene and others worry after, what Michel Foucault calls "the self", is left unattended. Perhaps it is unsurprising that students are disassociated from classrooms that "anesthetize learning" their bodies numbed by learned exclusion of sense experience. Students are disciplined by a discourse of knowledge that ignores the development of techniques of body/sense attention. The consequence is a missed opportunity for youth to learn to understand the role of sensuous knowledge in their physical realities along with the attendant and complex processes of signification that connect these sensations to meanings. Youth and teachers alike are instructed to silence their bodies (hooks, 1994, 113). Should it then surprise educators that students, after being implicitly or explicitly told to ignore the most obvious knowledge tool, wonder why they are attending school at all?

Anestheticized learning is education numbed to sensuous knowledge. It is learning that ignores affect in any form be it excitement, tension, passion, frustration or libidinal energies, let alone the senses and sensory signification as a form of knowledge. Learning numbed to sensuous knowledge ignores a full spectrum of lived experience and misses an opportunity to engage with theories of knowledge formation. But recognizing a current state of numbness is not the same as un-numbing it. We need to find methods to undo the pervasive educational anesthetic being injected into student's imaginations at epidemic levels. Aesthetic education, learning that attends to the body in community as a central engine for knowledge creation, is the best way to fight this.

CULTURAL STUDIES OF SENSIBILITY

So far I have used definitions of aesthetics focused on the Greek notion "sense perception or sensation" (Blumenfeld-Jones, 2012, 43). But this is not the only game in town. In fact as Theodore Adorno and more recently Jacques Rancière have pointed out, the discourse of aesthetics is a political terrain. Aesthetics— not the study of signification but the word itself—becomes signified as a set of characteristics of expressive practices, the possession of decorous objects, and a branch of philosophy that studies Art. A cultural studies of aesthetics (MacDonald, 2014) must therefore begin with a meta-analysis or deconstruction of the term aesthetics, not to illustrate its lack of meaning but its excess of meanings that leads to confusion on the subject.

In popular usage the phrase "the aesthetic characteristics of..." is so common that it seems unnecessary or perhaps unnatural to think deeply about it. It is as if Art possesses a set of characteristics that the aesthetic philosopher, often simply called the critic, can enumerate. It is the surface of things except when one accounts for the magical gaze of the critic. The critic is the traditional authority over aesthetics, the individual endowed with the capacity to "see", account for, or at least make visible the aesthetic criteria that makes any piece of art meaningful and therefore valuable. In a discussion of the tension between Aesthetics and Cultural Studies Winfried Fluck notes that:

> It [cultural studies] breaks down the barrier between high culture and popular or mass culture and says that both—that all cultural practices—are worth studying. What distinguished post-World War II literary studies from philology was that it was based on certain aesthetics norms. Not all works qualified for serious professional consideration, and a crucial, if not the crucial, task of the critic was to determine what works were legitimate objects of study. (2002, 83)

Aesthetics in this sense is a discussion of hierarchies and value(s) in either, or both, the cultural or economic senses of the term. Aesthetic education has been used for the establishment of cultural hierarchies through arts education, simply arts appreciation. This method has been successful for disseminating culturally valuable works, at least as defined by critics. Often this is the work that is allowed into the curriculum.

With the rise of Popular Music the critic has been replaced with the marketplace. Valuation has shifted from a supposed disinterested determination by an expert critic to valuation determined almost completely on an arts marketplace. Critics in the lineage of Adorno have argued that this shift to the culture industries has had profoundly negative effects. While I am not as willing as many in the Frankfurt School to demonize art business there are some obvious downsides to marketplace history. For instance, History of Popular Music textbooks are a collection of successfully marketed products with a historic value determined by their economic success either at the point of creation/release or (as is often the case) by later market valuation as a historically significant product. The role of the critic and the marketplace are two expressions of the institutional mechanics for the creation of aesthetic value. But aesthetic value is not the only social process, people do not engage in aesthetics only as an exchange of value. To use a Marxist political economic language there is not only exchange value but also use value. The use value of aesthetics is its aesthetic function.

Aesthetic function is an experience often mistakenly situated inside the work of art:

> The capacity of any system of signification to draw attention to itself as a form of expression and refers to itself as a sign, thus drawing our attention to the organization and patterning principles by which the object is constituted. For

119

this purpose, the object is temporarily depragmatized and dereferentialized…
this temporary bracketing of reference is useful and often gives pleasure, not
because it allows us to escape, if only temporarily, from reality but because
it opens up the possibility of a new perspective on the object which we have
missed in our exclusive concentration on the referential function. (Fluck, 2002,
87–88 emphasis added)

But there are no systems of signification that draw "attention to itself", there is
instead always a dynamic flow between a participating subject, a culture, and a sign
systems within which a work is organized and from which knowledge, in the form of
aesthetic experience, emerges as a singularity (Rancière; Foucault). The singularity is
the aesthetic experience (Dewey, Berleant). Unfortunately, Fluck avoids recognizing
the existence of aesthetic knowledge and yet cannot ignore that 'something' occurs.
So instead of researching the complexity of aesthetic function some writers prefer
an explanation that the work of art is endowed with special powers that allow 'it'
to produce affect and in the process of doing 'it' establishes a special substance that
only critics can make visible, the aesthetic. This approach needs to be resisted. A
step in resistance is to recognize that the aesthetic function might be the affective
impact of coming in contact with aesthetic knowledge. Following Joe Kincheloe's
explanation of Blues aesthetic-knowledge as Blue Epistemology (2005), I suggest
that what is required is not a reductivist or reified approach to aesthetic function but
instead a more complex cultural investigation of aesthetics as a study of culturally
produced and culturally shared knowledge formation, distribution and maintenance
(epistemology). The result of this approach is the need for a cultural studies of
aesthetics that I call, in short, Aesthetic Systems. Aesthetic education therefore is
not just learning about art but is instead learning about and developing an awareness
of the role of the senses and their signification in the production of knowledge within
a cultural context. Aesthetic education takes two roads. Either it is a pedagogy of
liberating knowledge production by inviting students to take their place as joint
producers of aesthetic knowledge or alternatively, and all too regularly, aesthetic
education used to dominate and discipline students' bodies by instructing students
on how they should or aught to understand/signify their senses.

AESTHETIC SYSTEMS AND THE CULTURE CIRCLE

As bell hooks noted in Yearnings (1990) thinking deeply about aesthetics is not
limited to philosophers and critics, but is rarely found in books. I was recently
reminded of this in conversation with a senior ethnomusicologist at an academic
conference. Trying to articulate my interest in aesthetic epistemology I used an
example that I thought would be meaningful to him. Drawing from a geographical
area he has been studying for more than two decades I asked where I might find a
written discussion of a term found in the discourse of culture members. He admitted
that although there is plenty written about how the music is made, little to nothing has

been written about the system of knowledge that supports the expressive practices. I understand this as an exclusion of aesthetic epistemology. Its exclusion occurs when aesthetic research remains at surface descriptions of practices without attention to knowledge that guides these techniques. The physical motion of dance, the notes sounded, the paint scratched or spread on medium silences, often unintentionally, a self that is busily carving out a new territory. This new space is subject-of-culture. While the same analytical discussion might suggest that agency is being enacted in the expressive practice, agency is cut down by surface descriptions. Aesthetic research methodology that does not include, in various registers, the voices of creative subjects limits and greatly simplifies knowledge contribution. Of course it is much easier to move towards knowledge reduction; to watch a performance, make a video document of it, make notes about it (even reflexive notes) and pose surface questions of participants. In fact you might resist what I am saying about the silencing of subjects by correctly pointing out that interviews provide an opportunity for creative subjects to voice their epistemological positions. But critical researchers have long been aware that discourse, because of its appearance as the common and the everyday, makes its functioning resistant to easy description even by participants. Aesthetic epistemology therefore requires the development of a method of research that provides a space for critical awareness, what might be called the development of cultural meta-analysis. For this I turn to Paulo Freire's Culture Circle.

In *Education for Critical Consciousness* (2005) Paulo Freire discusses the economic changes brought about in Brazil by the forces of rapid industrialization. Brazilian Educators were tasked with bringing literacy to illiterate communities to facilitate participation in industrialization. Freire realized however that teaching Portuguese to indigenous communities was not absent of politics, but instead was a continuation of colonization. Freire overturned the deficit of illiteracy by recognizing the powerful epistemologies embedded in non-literate cultures connected to complex cosmologies and grounded in environmental knowledge, now termed Traditional Ecological Knowledge (TEK). Freire's method, the culture circle, brought community members together to discuss and make explicit community knowledge. To do this he worked with a visual artist to create visual situations that would provide a context for the conversation. A facilitator brought the situation to the circle and worked with the circle to articulate, to make visible, knowledge of each situation. At the end of these twelve situations members of the circle began to see that literacy in Portuguese is a cultural technology that can be used to do work. Instead of being disciplined by a colonial language, formerly non-literate community members became critically multicultural in that they could function within non-literate epistemological and literate epistemological contexts. One might be reminded that according to discourse theory, "discourses fix meaning by excluding all other meaning potentials. Two discourses can collide in an antagonistic relationship to one another when they try to define the same terrain in conflicting ways" (Jorgensen, 2002, 190). Freire saw this an other way. He used the situation of conflicting discourse as a way of making knowable both the discourse possessed by the community as well as the colonial discourse. Instead of one discourse dominating the other, two discourses could be held together in a tension that contributes to developing critical consciousness. Drawing from this awareness I, along with Andre Hamilton, used a cultural formation from Hiphop Kulture, the cypher, to see if we could create a Hiphop Culture Circle.

CIPHER5: HIP HOP CONSCIENTIZATION AND OVERSTANDING

Cypher is a Hiphop circle in which hiphoppas freestyle or drop writtens (deliver prewritten rhymes) one after the other. Cypher also refers to a circle that forms to share other substance, sometimes marijuana. But cypher can also refer to an engagement with the subconscious in a stream-of-conscious delivery in rhyme. This kind of freestyle flow is often taken as a sign of mastery of the Hiphop element of emceeing, something I have previously called epistemological flow (MacDonald, 2012). Cipher, spelled with an i, refers to cryptography and processes of encryption and decryption. In this sense Cipher is recognition of the processes of signification and deconstruction that take place. Related to the cryptographic spelling of Cipher is our use of the number five, Cipher5. Five refers to knowledge as the fifth element of Hiphop Kulture after emceeing, graffiti, b-boying/b-girling, and Djing. Cipher5 is a cypher that brings together hiphoppas, with students, and professional researchers to produce and share knowledge about Hiphop Kulture. Cipher5 takes place every Tuesday night at 7pm at a local café. We have an arrangement with the café owner where we can organize chairs in a circle and make use of the sound system, projector, and computer for sharing videos, songs, and other online content related to Hiphop Kulture.

As implied by the name and built on Freire's use of 'situations' in the Culture Circle, Cipher5 works to make Hiphop knowledge visible to members. I am using visibility in the sense that Cipher5 is a critical method for making explicit the often-subjugated knowledge of Hiphop Kulture. This is cultural aesthetics, a practice of publicly producing aesthetic epistemology. But following Freire's situations required a translation process. It would simply not work to blindly follow the Culture Circle method. While the purpose of our Culture Circle, Cipher5, is indeed conscientização, conscientizing, or the raising of critical consciousness, our method had to make sense to us. Taking what may seem like a rather traditional approach we formed Cipher5 as a reading group in the basement of a local independent bookstore. It was an opportunity for local hiphoppas to gather to read The Gospel of Hiphop, "presented by" KRS-ONE (2009).

AN EMANCIPATORY BOOK CLUB

My passion for a reading group did not spring from my experiences in grad school (as you may at first suppose), but from my first book club, a 3am independent sci-fi circle at a now long closed Tim Horton's coffee shop in Sydney, Cape Breton, Canada. This requires a bit of a story to illustrate the two lessons I learned from the experience: First, youth need only an opportunity for critical engagement and rarely need to be introduced to the passion of learning (they simply need a space to unleash what they possess) and second, as Gramsci long ago noted, the critical revolutionary intellectual is not always found in a university classroom, but in the make-shift classrooms of the community.

I was a teenager working summer back-shift at a grocery store. Sometime in the middle of the summer my sleeping pattern had become flipped backwards, so that on my days off I had a hard time getting back to a daytime schedule. So instead of trying very hard I would often take a book and find an open coffee shop. I had no plan. I was not trying to read enough to get into graduate school. In fact no one in my family had attended graduate school so I did not yet know what the domestic practice of scholarship looked like, what the scholar does in their spare time. I have, what I now recognize to be, a long-term passion for knowledge and that this passion is a vital component of knowledge: "For Foucault, as for Plato after the symposium, knowledge must be seen as a genre of desire" (Steigler, 2010, 172). But at this point I had no words for this. All I knew was the pleasure of late night reading.

On one of these early morning adventures I walked into a coffee shop I had not yet visited. I purchased my coffee and, as was my habit, I headed for the corner where I would not be distracted by the activity at the counter. It was not long before I was interrupted by an increase in volume in the little shop. As was the case in all Tim Horton's of the time, there was a large square counter surrounded by stools that was called 'the island'. The island was full and was presided over by the very large security guard I passed when I walked into the shop. Now, however, he was transfigured. A large smile spread across his wide face softening the hard features of his large shaved head. He verbally poked the members of the group, pushing them to talk, coaxing them into debate. I guess I started to stare because it was not long before he was looking straight at me. I tried to break his gaze but he would have none of it. It was too late for me. He asked me what I was reading and shook his head with displeasure at my response. He called me over.

I was the youngest person at the table by at least fifteen years and I was not the focus of the conversation. I had unwittingly discovered an early morning book club—it was the Fight Club of book clubs really, but long before anyone would have that reference. Over that summer I was introduced to ideas and Nova Scotia sci-fi authors I had never heard of, and most importantly I learned in that circle what Culture Circle members likely learned with Freire, that the world of the mind is not out of reach, that knowledge is not owned or managed by an exclusive class of people. I also learned there is knowledge-of-self that can be gained in this rough community classroom, the one that you choose as the place to take a stand against a world constructed for you. It was in this coffee shop where I learned that making knowledge is an emancipatory act.

I now have more than 20 years distance on that classroom. Having had my first career in the music industry (and all of the classrooms that come with that life), and having also had the joys and pains of university seminars along the way on one's journey to a PhD, I have gained perspective. There is no one single classroom that can teach all of the lessons that we will learn. And it seems that certain lessons come along with certain classrooms. With this in mind I partnered with Andre Hamilton to create a reading circle as situation or singularity that we call Cipher5.

Hamilton and I followed the lessons I learned at that coffee shop, and the ones he learned in a lifetime of Hiphop Kulture and we understood them through the lens of critical pedagogy and my newer teachers hooks, Steinberg, Kincheloe, Freire, Maclaren, and Giroux. The situation is the reading circle and the context, and the Gospel of Hip-Hop is often but perhaps not always, the subject. After the ritual introduction necessary so everyone in the circle hears their own voice and is heard by the subjects that form the circle, we may only read two lines. Where the conversation goes after these lines are spoken is unknown. We have no curriculum and no timeline. We have been meeting for eighteen months as of April 2014 and have yet to read the entire book. Some sections, like the Hiphop Declaration of Peace have been read more than a dozen times because it is a collection of eighteen principles that hiphoppas are encouraged to live by. The Fifth Overstanding: The Inner City and the Thirteenth Overstanding: The Hip Hop Activist have also been read a number of times. But even these sections have not been completely read within the circle. Sections are recited, sometimes cypher style, each paragraph read by a different member of the circle, with books getting passed around.

And often the Gospel of Hip Hop does not even get opened. Someone may come with a video or a section of lyrics for discussion. Perhaps a documentary such as the United States of Africa, or Ice T's The Art of Rap will be the focus. But whatever the focus, the process is the same; we come together to articulate our questions, forward our ideas, practice our critical thinking and leave the Cipher excited and engaged with a more fully realized passion for knowledge.

CIPHER5: METHOD FOR RESEARCH AND TEACHING

The practice of Cipher5 provides a way of practicing critical pedagogy as a model for critical research. At the root is a dismissal or a denial of the two sidedness of the project, or put another way, a denial of the distance between research and education. Research is learning. Arne De Boever (2011) takes the denial a step further by denying a distance between research and philosophy. It comes down to the statement "philosophy is education: that it was and has always been education, since its beginning in Ancient Greece" (34). The practice of generating knowledge in Cipher5 is philosophy practiced by hiphoppas, it is the work of articulating the practices/art of living that Michel Foucault identifies as culture. Philosophy in this view is the articulation and evaluation of a mode of life, not the professional practice of an intellectual elite. Cipher5 started as a way of generating research about hip-hop, hip-hop as the manifestation of Hiphop Kulture, and became the practice of articulating the practices of Kulture, and therefore a form of philosophy classroom. Through Cipher5 we rediscovered a practical philosophy, or at least a renegade philosophy that occurs in the street, the kind of philosophy that Jacques Rancière calls political because it creates an opportunity for those without voice to learn to speak: "My vision of philosophy is first of all a vision of thought as a power of declassification, of the redistribution of territorial divisions among disciplines and competences. Philosophy says that thought belongs to all. It says this, though, at the very moment that it states division and exclusions" (2011, 23). Cipher5 calls our process creation of knowledge but stops short of naming ourselves philosophers or a philosophical community. Perhaps this is an expression of power that must be undone.

But we also do not call Cipher5 a classroom even though it does the work of education. Gert Biesta in "Toward a New "Logic" of Emancipation: Foucault and Rancière" writes that:

The idea of emancipation plays a central role in modern education. To the extent that education is about more than the transmission of content and culture but involves an interest in fostering independence and autonomy, education can be said to be a process that aims at the emancipation of the child or the student. (169)

If education is defined this way and not defined by the institutionalization of learning then we are free to study organized learning or the practice of community philosophy in any environment equally. Cipher5—as my research assistants maintain in autoethnographic works I will draw from below—is a practice of philosophy and complex practice of self-knowledge and care-of-the-self points towards emancipation. It seems that cultural research-as-education works because it generates community knowledge of the forces of power that are experienced by members of the circle, who are free and encouraged by peers to speak their narratives. As Biesta notes: "The key idea is that emancipation can be brought about if people gain adequate insight into the power relations that constitute their situation – which is why the notion of demystification plays such a central role in critical pedagogies" (171) but as Freire pointed out if the pedagogue arrives to be savior then his very presence assures the learner will never be emancipated, but will fall under the authority of the teacher/critic, the one endowed with the magic power to de-mystify. But this practice leads to the emergence of another ideological power evident in Marxist notions of 'false consciousness' that has remained present in Critical Theory which Biesta calls the 'predicament of ideology':

The "predicament of ideology" lies in the suggestion that it is precisely because of the way in which power works upon our consciousness, that we are unable to see how the power works upon our consciousness. This not only implies that in order to free ourselves from the working of power we need to expose how power works upon our consciousness. It also means that in order for us to achieve emancipation, someone else, whose consciousness is not subjected to the workings of power, needs to provide us with an account of our objective condition. (171)

But the critical consciousness in the Freirian mode calls forth something altogether different. It relies on community-produced knowledge, or more precisely on the effect of community-produced knowledge. In our formulation the collective act of philosophy-of-culture that we practice in Cipher5 places the development of consciousness in the center of an increasingly critical discussion. The effectiveness of this, as Freire also showed, is the simultaneous articulation of community knowledge and individual emancipation. Jacques Rancière, in *The Ignorant Schoolmaster: Five Lessons in Intellectual Emancipation*, explains this process in another context.

Rancière tells the incredible story of a quiet teacher and former French revolutionary Deputy forced to flee to the Netherlands on the return of the monarchy and the pedagogical adventure he unexpectedly undertook. The adventure begins with the fact that Joseph Jacotot could not speak any Flemish and the students he was tasked to work with spoke no French. So instead of providing educational lessons he provided a book with a translation and let the students do the work. He expected little "he had believed what all conscientious professors believe: that the important business of the master is to transmit his knowledge to his students so as to bring them, by degrees, to his own level of expertise" (Rancière, 1991, 3). So it was with great surprise that the students learned to read and write French and "the logic of the explicative system had to be overturned. Explication is not necessary to remedy an incapacity to understand" (ibid. 6) and in fact "before being the act of the pedagogue, explication is the myth of pedagogy, the parable of a world divided into knowing minds and ignorant ones, ripe minds and immature ones, the capable and the incapable, the intelligent and the stupid" (Rancière, 1991, 6). Explication is not without power, according to Rancière (and Jacotot), "explication is not only the stultifying weapon of pedagogues but the very bond of the social order. Whoever says order says distribution into ranks. Putting into ranks presupposes explication, the distributory, justificatory fiction of an inequality that has no other reason for being" (ibid., 117).

Cipher5 is not however built on Jacotot's nor Rancière model. It developed from my book club adventure and from of our practice of Hiphop Kulture (MacDonald, 2012, 2014). It was the impact of the socially produced knowledge at Cipher5 that left me looking for answers and explications that led me to intellectual emancipation, Foucault, Rancière, and Jacotot. And while I resisted drawing from these sources to explain my experience at Cipher5 it occurred to me that enforcing this separation maintained the divisions between philosophy (including aesthetics), education, and cultural practice. This chapter is an act of tearing down these walls and confirming that living Hiphop Kulture is the act of living aesthetically, philosophically.

CIPHER5 AS LEARNING MODEL IN STUDENT'S OWN WORDS

One of the joys of running a Participatory Action Research circle is that you have a constant engagement in knowledge production. This year I began a new position as an assistant professor at a new university in a faculty of fine arts with no legacy of social science research. This was the first time that students from this department worked as research assistants and I was very interested what kind of impact their participation would have on their intellectual and scholarly development. I was cautious to choose RAs knowing that their level of engagement would, in some ways, lay the foundation for the near future. I decided to wait to see which students would attend the Hiphop Kulture symposium I organized in the first semester. As it turned out, two students volunteered and showed up for everything. They made the decision easy. Soon after the symposium I began the process of hiring them as research assistants to support Cipher5. Their assignment was to attend Cipher5 and to take notes over the semester. At the end of the semester they were asked to provide an autoethnography of their experience. Once the autoethnography was written and submitted the three of us sat down and discussed their experience. I only then mentioned that I was interested in exploring Cipher5 as a form of classroom and that they, in fact, were the first students. I asked them to go back over their autoethnographies to produce another layer of analysis, this time identifying the connection between events and their own learning. What follows is a series of examples of their work. It is necessary to include their voice because it provides the evidence of the functioning of Cipher5 as both a research circle and as a form of emancipatory pedagogy.

Student 1:

- The open nature (circle) of the Cipher works to break down the idea that there is one all-knowing teacher who speaks to students who are inferior. I love this learning model, because what I'm experiencing is that good communication is a great tool for more thorough learning.
- I feel the circle has helped build my own confidence. I don't feel it gives me an ego boost; rather, exploring abstract topics that have many sides (spirituality, sexuality, religion, mainstream music) or points of view is a great opportunity to allow yourself to be scared and state your opinion anyway. I think it's important for members of the circle to remain open-minded, to be patient as listeners and not always feel the need to be right.
- The circle really gives its members a chance to share their own personal history and experience, which may be essential to the healthy development of our identities. It seems to be a therapeutic place where there is compassion for everyone's stories, which I think allows for healing.
- I had some really positive feelings tonight. For me, the community/welcoming aspect of the cipher keeps developing. It's starting to feel like a soccer team you join half-heartedly simply because your friend invited you and you committed to the first game. Before you know it you wouldn't even dream of missing a practice, let alone a game. This is the feeling of community. I don't necessarily yet know my role or the extent of my contribution to the Cipher, but I feel like my role and contribution not only exists, but is a stepping stone to further awareness and

education around social issues. I have a place and when I look around the circle, everyone has a place. We are working towards a common vision, and there are so many facets to that vision (so many different backgrounds, motives, experiences that blend together beautifully). Each time I take part in the Cipher, I think more and more about identity—both of others and my own. The sense of direction (or misdirection) an identity brings impacts our lives every day. Who we think we are, the kinds of things we believe in or don't believe in, the habits we form, etc. I feel like maybe my sense of identity hasn't been true to what I actually WANT and aspire to have in my life. This circle (through reflection) is helping me to form a more solid identity of myself. I don't know yet know what that identity consists of.

- Tonight a First Nations hiphoppa told us that when he was growing up as a first nations youth, he felt society already looked upon him as scum so he felt like being poor and dealing drugs was of no further shame to him or his identity, whereas with middle-class (white) society they would never want to be caught dead selling drugs. But once Hiphop glamorized it, suddenly it became "cool" and "badass" to do drugs. I think this argument and image of drug use has been around for years, if not centuries. That was a sad story for me to hear. I feel angry hearing about the racist mindset towards First Nations people (and any race). Often when a First Nations Canadian tells me a story about the injustice of their struggles, I am filled with rage and want to pursue this story of furthered colonialism. This thought brought me to the appreciation of our path in life. Six months ago, I never would have guessed I'd be attending weekly Hip Hop community circles discussing social and political and racial issues. This is amazing. My mother told me that going to school is never a waste of money. I was questioning whether that was true, but in this moment I am not necessarily thankful that I study music every day. I am thankful that I'm in the position where I am becoming exposed to higher levels of thinking, philosophy, and desire for social change. That's what I want to be a part of my life.

Student 2:

- Each time I attend, I always feel like I have so much to learn but instead of being discouraged with how much information there is in the world (which I often do at school/in a classroom environment), I feel inspired to continue listening to peoples' stories and to absorb as much as I can through this community.
- Through this reflection process I have developed a deeper understanding of myself: my social, political, musical, and religious positions, as well as a critical evaluation of these beliefs. This has been both a learning opportunity and a challenge as I am dissecting my preconceived ideas of identity and challenging certain aspects that I do not like, such as those beliefs that do not fit into this new cultural group, or those that I no longer value and am struggling to let go of. There is a personal identity crisis going on: I am evaluating who I have become, what

environmental elements have contributed to that formulation of self and whether or not that is somebody I want to continue to be. These questions and concerns are a direct result of the unique personal, transformative qualities of engaging in this method. This ties into the challenge and conflict of racial identity and prejudice. A huge challenge for me has been confronting prejudices I was not previously aware of, that were in my subconscious mind affecting my conscious behavior.

• Through this process, my ignorance of the cultural, political and social history of a marginalized group of people has been exposed. A unique element of this method is the development of relationship-based learning to generate this knowledge and awareness.

• This is a completely different model of education. It is an exchange and sharing of personal stories where the self is not divorced from the learning, it is an integral component. This brings up a unique set of challenges in the learning environment: trust between participants, a willingness and openness to share, express vulnerability, to be challenged, and potentially exposed in one's lack of knowledge and/or difference of opinion. The relationships formed provide the opportunity for the creation of a deeper level of understanding, acknowledging the emotional, physical, spiritual, social, economic ingredients that make up a community and a culture.

CONCLUSIONS

So while there are a variety of levels of success in this method, there are some challenges presenting themselves as well. The realization of Cipher5 as youth activism, research and pedagogical space requires a more thorough investigation of my practices. What role have I played in preparing the research assistants for their participation, and how might I fit this role into the model? The RAs were certainly not left alone to deal with their process, in fact the research practice required, or at least provided a context for, the development of strong ties between RAs and myself as principle investigator. Further elaboration of these dynamics is required before too much more can be said about the value of Cipher5 as a teaching environment. Relatedly, it is necessary to evaluate how the rest of the community members of Cipher5 feel about contributing to student learning; what is the reciprocal contribution to the community? In my opening example of the security guards at the Tim Horton's coffee shop, it seems like he was making community by sharing knowledge and sharing the creation of knowledge. But of course he was also getting paid to be there and the draw of the reading circle made certain that there were bodies in the coffee shop late at night keeping him company. Likely, the mechanics of community are much more complex than we have yet addressed. Therefore, and in these directions, the research will continue. We will continue to publish articles about Hiphop Kulture in our city but we will now also publish about alternative learning environments, new approaches to community philosophy, and emancipation.

CHAPTER 8

NOTE

[1] Originally published as "Cipher5 as Method in Hiphop Kulture Research: Developing a Critical Community-Engaged Research Method for a Cultural Studies of Music". In *Research Methods for Critical Youth Studies*, Awad Ibrahim and Shirley R. Steinberg (Eds.), Peter Lang Publishing, New York, 2015. Reprinted with permission.

REFERENCES

Adorno, T. W. (1976). *Introduction to the sociology of music* (E. B. Ashton, Trans.). New York, NY: The Seabury Press. (Original work published 1962)

Adorno, T. W. (1984). *Aesthetic theory* (C. Lenhardt, Trans., G. Adorno & R. Tiedmann, Eds.). Boston, MA: Routledge & Kegan Paul. (Original work published 1970)

Adorno, T. W. (1991). *The culture industry: Selected essays on a mass culture* (J. M. Bernstein, Ed.). New York, NY: Routledge.

Adorno, T. W., Benjamin, W., Bloch, E., Brecht, B., & Lukacs, G. (1977). *Aesthetics and politics.* New York, NY: Verso.

Alcoff, L. M. (2007). Mignolo's epistemology of coloniality. *CR: The New Centennial Review, 7*(3), 79–101.

Arnold, M. (1932). *Culture and anarchy.* New York, NY: Cambridge University Press.

Arribas-Ayllon, M., & Walkerdine, V. (2008). Foucauldian discourse analysis. In C. Willig & W. Stainton-Rogers (Eds.), *The Sage handbook of qualitative research in psychology* (pp. 91–108). Thousand Oaks, CA: Sage Publications.

Attali, J. (1999). *Noise: The political economy of music* (B. Massumi, Trans.). Minneapolis, MN: University of Minnesota Press.

Baraka, A. (1973). *Black art.* New York, NY: Morrow.

Baraka, A., & Harris, W. J. (1991). *The LeRoi Jones/Amiri Baraka reader.* New York, NY: Thunder's Mouth Press.

Basso, K. H. (1996). Wisdom sits in places: Notes on a Western Apache landscape. In S. Feld & K. H. Basso (Eds.), *Senses of place,* Santa Fe, NM: School of American Research Press.

Bateson, G. (1972). *Steps to an ecology of mind.* Chicago, IL: University of Chicago Press.

Battiste, M. (2013). *Decolonizing education: Nourishing the learning spirit.* Saskatoon, SK: Purich Publishing.

Baucom, I. (2001). Frantz Fanon's radio: Solidarity, diaspora, and the tactics of listening. *Contemporary Literature, 42*(1), 15–49.

Baudrillard, J. (1981). *For a critique of the political economy of the sign.* St. Louis, MO: Telos Press.

Baudrillard, J. (1996). *The system of objects* (J. Benedict, Trans.). New York, NY: Verso.

Bauman, Z. (1982). *Memories of class: The pre-history and after-life of class.* London, UK: Routledge & Kegan Paul.

Bauman, Z. (1999). *In search of politics.* Stanford, CA: Stanford University Press.

Bauman, Z. (2011). *Culture in a liquid modern world.* Cambridge, UK: Polity Press.

Becker, C., Crawford, R., & Miller, P. D. (2002). An interview with Paul D. Miller a.k.a. Dj Spooky—That subliminal kid. *Art Journal, 61*(1), 82–91.

Becker, H. S. (1984). *Art worlds.* Berkeley, CA: University of California Press.

Beisswenger, D. (2002). *Fiddling way out yonder: The life and music of Melvin Wine.* Jackson, MS: University Press of Mississippi.

Benjamin, W. (1968). The work of art in the age of mechanical reproduction (H. Zohn, Trans.). In A. Hannah (Ed.), *Illuminations* (pp. 219–253). New York, NY: Harcourt Brace & World.

Benston, K. W. (2000). *Performing blackness: Enactments of African-American modernism.* New York, NY: Routledge.

Berleant, A. (1991). *Art and engagement.* Philadelphia, PA: Temple University Press.

Berleant, A. (1992). *The aesthetics of environment.* Philadelphia, PA: Temple University Press.

Berleant, A. (1999). Getting along beautifully: Ideas for a social aesthetics. In P. Von Bonsdorff & A. Haapala (Eds.), *Aesthetics in the human environment* (Vol. 6, pp. 12–29). Lahti, Finland: International Institute for Applied Aesthetics.

Berleant, A. (2000). *The aesthetic field.* New York, NY: Cybereditions.

REFERENCES

Berleant, A. (2002). Notes for a cultural aesthetic. In V. Sarapik, K. Tüür, & M. Laanemets (Eds.), *Koht ja paik* [Place and location] (pp. 19–26). Tallinn, Estonia: Eesti Kunstiakadeemia (Estonian Academy of Arts).

Berleant, A. (2004). *Re-thinking aesthetics: Rogue essays on aesthetics and the arts.* Aldershot, UK: Ashgate.

Berleant, A. (2005). *Aesthetics and environment: Variation on a theme.* Burlington, VT: Ashgate Publishing Inc.

Berleant, A. (2010). *Sensibility and sense: The aesthetic transformation of the human world.* Charlottesville, VA: Imprint Academic.

Bérubé, M. (2005). *The aesthetics of cultural studies.* Malden, MA: Blackwell.

Besley, T., & Peters, M. A. (2007). *Subjectivity and truth: Foucault, education, and the culture of self.* New York, NY: Peter Lang.

Beynon, C. A., & Veblen, K. K. (2012). *Critical perspectives in Canadian music education.* Waterloo, ON: Wilfred Laurier University Press.

Blumenfeld-Jones, D. S. (2012). *Curriculum and the aesthetic life: Hermeneutics, body, democracy, and ethics in curriculum theory and practice.* New York, NY: Peter Lang.

Blunden, A. (2013). Contradiction, consciousness, and generativity: Hegel's roots in Freire's work. In R. Lake & T. Kress (Eds.), *Paulo Freire's intellectual roots: Towards historicity in praxis* (pp. 11–28). New York, NY: Bloomsbury.

Boal, A. (2006). *The aesthetics of the oppressed* (A. Jackson, Trans.). New York, NY: Routledge.

Bourriaud, N. (2002). *Relational aesthetics* (S. Pleasance, F. Woods, & M. Copeland, Trans.). Dijon, France: Les Presses du réel.

Bowie, A. (1990). *Aesthetics and subjectivity: From Kant to Nietzsche.* New York, NY: Manchester University Press.

Bowman, W. (1993). The problem of aesthetics and multiculturalism in music education. *Canadian Music Educator, 34*(5), 23–31.

Brew, A., & Boud, D. (1995). Teaching and research: Establishing the vital link with learning. *Higher Education, 29*(3), 261–273.

Caponi, G. D. (Ed.). (1999). *Signifyin(g), sanctifyin', & slam dunking: A reader in African American expressive culture.* Amherst, MA: University of Massachusetts Press.

Carr, W., & Kemmis, S. (1986). *Becoming critical: Education, knowledge and action research.* London: Falmer.

Chamberland, R. (2001). Rap in Canada: Bilingual and multicultural. In T. Mitchell (Ed.), *Global noise* (pp. 306–323). Middleton, CT: Wesleyan University Press.

Chion, M. (1994). *Audio-vision: Sounds on screen* (C. Gorbman, Trans.). New York, NY: Columbia University Press.

Christen, R. S. (2010). Graffiti as a public educator of urban teenagers. In J. A. Brian, D. Schultz Sandlin, & J. Burdick (Eds.), *Handbook of public pedagogy.* New York, NY: Routledge.

Clarke, E. F. (2005). *Ways of listening: An ecological approach to the perception of musical meaning.* New York, NY: Oxford University Press.

Cohen, D. B. (2005). Towards a performance-based pedagogy of self-determination. In J. Crowther, V. Galloway, & I. Martin (Eds.), *Popular education: Engaging the academy: International perspectives.* Leicester, UK: National Institute of Adult Continuing Education.

Crain, T. M. (2014). Beyond coverage: Teaching for understanding in the music history survey classroom. *Journal of Music History Pedagogy, 4*(2), 301–318.

Cremin, L. (1988). *American education: The metropolitan experience, 1876–1980.* New York, NY: Harper and Row.

Cruz, A. L. (2013). Paulo Freire's concept of conscientização. In R. Lake & T. Kress (Eds.), *Paulo Freire's intellectual roots: Towards historicity in praxis* (pp. 169–182). New York, NY: Bloomsbury.

Dallek, R. (1984). *Ronald Reagan: The politics of symbolism.* Cambridge, MA: Harvard University Press.

Daspit, T., & J. A. Weaver. (1999). Popular culture and critical pedagogy: Reading, constructing, connecting. In J. L. Kincheloe & S. R. Steinberg (Eds.), *Pedagogy and popular culture.* New York, NY: Garland Publishing.

De Boever, A. (2011). The philosophy of (aesthetic) education. In J. E. Smith & A. Weisser (Eds.), *Everything is in everything: Jacques Rancière between intellectual emancipation and aesthetic education* (pp. 34–48). New York, NY: Art Center Graduate Press.

DeLanda, M. (2006). *A new philosophy of society: Assemblage theory and social complexity.* New York, NY: Continuum.

DeLanda, M. (2006). Deleuzian social ontology and assemblage theory. In M. Fuglsang & B. Meier Sørensen (Eds.), *Deleuze and the social* (pp. 250–266). Edinburgh, UK: Edinburgh University Press.

Deleuze, G., & Guattari, F. (1983). *Anti-Oedipus: Capitalism and schizophrenia* (R. Hurley, M. Seem, & H. R. Lane, Trans.). Minneapolis, MN: The University of Minnesota Press.

Deleuze, G., & Guattari, F. (1987). *A thousand plateaus: Capitalism and schizophrenia* (B. Massumi, Trans.). Minneapolis, MN: University of Minnesota Press.

Dell'Antonio, A. (2004). *Beyond structural listening? Postmodern modes of hearing.* Berkley, CA: University of California Press.

Dewey, J. (1916). *Democracy and education.* New York, NY: Free Press.

Dewey, J. (1934). *Art as experience.* New York, NY: Capricorn Books.

Dewey, J. (1938). *Experience and education.* New York, NY: Macmillan.

Driscoll, M. P. (1994). *Psychology of learning for instruction.* Boston, MA: Allyn and Bacon.

Du Bois, W. E. B. (1994). *The souls of Black folk.* New York, NY: Dover.

Dunn, B. (2009). *Global political economy: A Marxist critique.* London, UK: Pluto Press.

Elliot, D. J. (1995). *Music matters.* New York, NY: Oxford University Press.

Elliott, E., Caton, L. F., & Rhyne, J. (2002). *Aesthetics in a multicultural age.* New York, NY: Oxford University Press.

Fechner, G. (1998). Aesthetics from above and from below (J. Gaiger, Trans.). In C. Harrison & P. Wood (Eds.), *Art in theory: 1815–1900* (pp. 633–636). London: Blackwell.

Feld, S. (1982). *Sound and sentiment: Birds, weeping, poetics, and song in Kaluli expression* (2nd ed.). Philadelphia, PA: University of Pennsylvania Press.

Fenster, M. (1989). Preparing the audience, informing the performers: John A. Lomax and cowboy songs and other frontier ballads. *American Music, 7*(3), 260–277.

Filene, B. (1991). Our singing country: John and Alan Lomax, Leadbelly, and the construction of an American past. *American Quarterly, 43*(4), 602–624.

Fine, E. H. (1971). Mainstream, blackstream and the Black art movement. *Art Journal, 30*(4), 374–375.

Fine, M., & Torre, M. E. (2008). Theorizing audience, products and provocation. In P. Reason & H. Bradbury (Eds.), *The Sage handbook of action research* (pp. 407–419). London: Sage.

Folkestad, G. (2000). Editorial. *International Journal of Music Education, 36*(1), 1–3.

Forman, M. (2000). 'Represent': Race, space and place in rap music. *Popular Music, 19*(1), 65–90.

Forney, K., & Machlis, J. (2007). *The enjoyment of music: An introduction to perceptive listening* (10th ed.). New York, NY: W.W. Norton.

Foucault, M. (1972). *The archaeology of knowledge: And the discourse on language.* New York, NY: Vintage Books.

Foucault, M. (1977). *Discipline and punish: The birth of the prison.* New York, NY: Vintage Books.

Foucault, M. (1980). *Power/Knowledge: Selected interviews and other writings 1972–1977.* New York, NY: Vintage Books.

Foucault, M. (1988). Technologies of the self. In L. H. Martin, H. Gutman, & P. H. Hutton (Eds.), *Technologies of the self.* Boston, MA: University of Massachusetts Press.

Foucault, M. (1994). *The order of things: An archaeology of the human sciences.* New York, NY: Vintage Books.

Foucault, M. (2004). *The hermeneutics of the subject: Lectures at the College de France 1981–1982.* New York, NY: Picador.

Foucault, M. (2010). *The government of self and others: Lectures at the College de France 1982–1983.* New York, NY: Palgrave MacMillan.

Freire, A. M. A., & Macedo, D. (Eds.). (1998). *The Paulo Freire reader.* New York, NY: Continuum.

Freire, P. (1970). *Pedagogy of the oppressed* (M. B. Ramos, Trans.). New York, NY: Continuum.

Freire, P. (2001). *Pedagogy of freedom: Ethics, democracy, and civic courage.* Lanham, MA: Rowman & Littlefield.

Freire, P. (2010). *Education for a critical consciousness*. New York, NY: Continuum.

Frith, S. (1981). *Sound effects: Youth, leisure, and the politics of rock 'n' roll*. New York, NY: Pantheon.

Gerstin, J. (1998). Reputation in a musical scene: The everyday context of connections between music, identity and politics. *Ethnomusicology, 42*(3), 385–414.

Gilroy, P. (1993). *The Black atlantic; Modernity and double consciousness*. Cambridge, MA: Harvard University Press.

Giroux, H. A. (1997). *Pedagogy and the politics of hope: Theory, culture, and schooling: A critical reader*. Boulder, CO: Westview Press.

Giroux, H. A. (2000). Public pedagogy as cultural politics: Stuart Hall and the 'crisis' of culture. *Cultural Studies, 14*(2), 341–360.

Giroux, H. A. (2003). *The abandoned generation: Democracy beyond the culture of fear*. New York, NY: Palgrave Macmillan.

Giroux, H. A. (2004). Public pedagogy and the politics of neo-liberalism: Making the political more pedagogical. *Policy Futures in Education, 2*(3–4), 494–503.

Giroux, H. A. (2009). *Youth in a suspect society: Democracy or disposability?* New York, NY: Palgrave MacMillan.

Gladney, M. J. (1995). The Black arts movement and hip-hop. *African American Review, 29*(2), 291–301.

Goertzen, C. (1997). *Fiddling for Norway: Revival and identity*. Chicago, IL: The University of Chicago Press.

Gordon, D. R., & Suits, D. B. (2003). *Epicurus: His continuing influence and contemporary relevance*. Rochester, NY: Rochester Institute of Technology Press.

Gordon, E. E. (1997). *Learning sequences in music: Skill, content, and patterns – A music learning theory*. Chicago, IL: GIA Publications, Inc.

Gramit, D. (2002). *Cultivating music: The aspirations, interests, and limits of German musical culture, 1770–1848*. Berkeley, CA: University of California Press.

Gray, H. (1995). *Watching race: Television and the struggle for Blackness*. Minneapolis, MN: University of Minnesota Press.

Green, L. (2008). *Music, informal learning, and the school: A new classroom pedagogy*. Burlington, VT: Ashgate.

Grossberg, L. (2010). *Cultural studies in the future tense*. Durham, NC: Duke University Press.

Guattari, F., & Rolnik, S. (2008). *Molecular revolution in Brazil*. Los Angeles, CA: Semiotext(e).

Guyer, P. (2005). *Values of beauty: Historical essays in aesthetics*. New York, NY: Cambridge University Press.

Harvey, D. (2005). *A brief history of neoliberalism*. New York, NY: Oxford University Press.

Hebert, D. G., & Campbell, P. S. (2000). Rock music in American schools: Positions and practices since the 1960s. *International journal of music education, 36*(1), 14–22.

Hegel, G. W. F. (1975). *Hegel's aesthetics: Lectures on fine arts* (T. M. Know, Trans.). Oxford: Claredon Press.

Henderson, E. A. (1996). Black nationalism and rap music. *Journal of Black Studies, 26*(3), 308–339.

Hill, S. J., & Ramsaran, D. (2009). *Hiphop and inequality: Searching for the "real" Slim Shady*. Amherst, NY: Cambria Press.

Hobsbawm, E. (1975). *The age of capital 1848–1875*. London, UK: Abacus.

Hoch, D. (2006). *Towards a hip-hop aesthetic: A manifesto for the hip-hop arts movement*. New York, NY: Hemispheric Institute.

hooks, b. (1990). *Yearning: Race, gender, and cultural politics*. Boston, MA: South End Press.

hooks, b. (1994). *Teaching to transgress: Education as the practice of freedom*. New York, NY: Routledge.

hooks, b. (2003). *Teaching community: A pedagogy of hope*. New York, NY: Routledge.

hooks, b. (2004). *The will to change: Men, masculinity, and love*. New York, NY: Atria Books.

hooks, b. (2008). *Belonging: A culture of place*. New York, NY: Routledge.

hooks, b. (2010). *Teaching critical thinking: Practical wisdom*. New York, NY: Routledge.

hooks, b. (2013). *Writing beyond race: Living theory and practice*. New York, NY: Routledge.

Horkheimer, M., & Adorno, T. W. (2002). *Dialectic of enlightenment: Philosophical fragments* (E. F. N. Jephcott, Trans., C. Godde Ed.). Stanford, CA: Stanford University Press. (Original work published 1947)

Hutton, P. H. (1988). Foucault, Freud, and the technologies of the self. In L. H. Martin, H. Gutman, & P. H. Hutton (Eds.), *Technologies of the self*. Boston, MA: University of Massachusetts Press.

Ibrahim, A. E. K. M. (1999). Becoming Black: Rap and hip-hop, race, gender, identity, and the politics of ESL learning. *TESOL Quarterly, 33*(3), 349–369.

Ibrahim, A., & Steinberg, S. R. (2014). *Critical youth studies reader.* New York, NY: Peter Lang.

Impey, A. (2002). Culture, conservation and community reconstruction: Explorations in participatory action research and advocacy ethnomusicology in the Dukuduku forests, Northern KwaZulu Natal (South Africa). *Yearbook for Traditional Music, 34,* 9–24.

Jelinek, A. (2013). *This is not art: Activism and other not-art.* London: JB Tauris & Co.

Jones, L. (1968). *Black music.* New York, NY: William Morrow.

Kapferer, J. (2008). *The State and the arts: Articulating power and subversion.* New York, NY: Berghahn Books.

Kapilow, R. (2008). *All you have to do is listen: Music from the inside out.* Hoboken, NJ: John Wiley and Sons.

Keil, C., & Feld, S. (1994). *Music grooves.* Chicago, IL: The University of Chicago Press.

Kendall, G., & Wickham, G. (1999). *Using Foucault's methods: Producing qualitative methods.* Thousand Oaks, CA: Sage Publications.

Kerman, J., & Tomlinson, G. (2008). *Listen.* Boston, MA: Bedford/St. Martin's.

Keyes, C. (2002). *Rap music and street consciousness.* Urbana, IL: University of Illinois Press.

Kincheloe, J. (2008). *Knowledge and critical pedagogy: An introduction.* New York, NY: Springer.

Kincheloe, J. L. (2005). *Critical constructivism.* New York, NY: Peter Lang.

Kincheloe, J. L. (2010). *Knowledge and critical pedagogy.* New York, NY: Springer.

Klein, D. (2012). The art of happiness introduction. In *Epicurus: The art of happiness* (G. K. Strodach, Trans.). New York, NY: Penguin Books.

Krims, A. (2000). *Rap music and the poetics of identity.* New York, NY: Cambridge University Press.

KRS ONE. (2009). *The gospel of Hip Hop: First instrument presented by KRS ONE for the Temple of Hip Hop.* Brooklyn, NY: Powerhouse Books.

Kun, J. (2005). *Audiotopia: Music, race and America.* Berkeley, CA: University of California Press.

Kuper, A. (2003). *Culture: The anthropologists' account.* Cambridge, MA: Harvard University Press.

Lacher, H. (2006). *Beyond globalization: Capitalism, territoriality and the international relations of modernity.* New York, NY: Routledge.

Lake, R., & Dagostino, V. (2013). Converging self/other awareness: Erich Fromm and Paulo Freire on transcending the fear of freedom. In R. Lake & T. Kress (Eds.), *Paulo Freire's intellectual roots: Towards historicity in Praxis* (pp. 101–126). New York, NY: Bloomsbury.

LeCourt, D. (2004). *Identity matters: Schooling the student body in academic discourse.* Albany, NY: State University of New York.

Lentin, A., & Titley, G. (2011). *The crises of multiculturalism: Racism in a neoliberal age.* New York, NY: Zed Books.

Low, S. (2005). *Theorizing the city: The new urban anthropology reader.* New Brunswick, NJ: Rutgers University Press.

Luhmann, N. (2000). *Art as a social system.* Stanford, CA: Stanford University Press.

MacDonald, M. B. (2012). Hip-hop citizens: Local hip-hop and the production of democratic grassroots change in Alberta. In B. J. Porfilio & M. J. Viola (Eds.), *Hip-hop(e): The cultural practice and critical pedagogy of international hip-hop* (pp. 95–109). New York, NY: Peter Lang.

MacDonald, M. B. (2014). A pedagogy of cultural sustainability: YEGH3 (Edmonton Hip-Hop history) as a decentralized model for Hip-Hop's global microhistories. In B. J. Porfilio, D. Roychoudhurry, & L. M. Gardner (Eds.), *See you at the crossroads: Dialectical harmony, ethics, aesthetics, and panoply of voices* (pp. 29–42). Rotterdam, The Netherlands: Sense Publishers.

MacDonald, M. B. (2014). Cultural studies of youth culture aesthetics as critical aesthetic education. In A. Ibrahim & S. R. Steinberg (Eds.), *Critical youth studies reader* (pp. 434–443). New York, NY: Peter Lang Press.

Macleod, C., & Bhatia, S. (2008). Postcolonialism and psychology. In C. Willig & W. Stainton-Rogers (Eds.), *The sage handbook of qualitative research in psychology* (pp. 576–589). Thousand Oaks, CA: Sage Publications.

Mallot, C., & Pena, M. (2004). Punk rockers' revolution: A pedagogy of race, class, and gender. In J. L. Kincheloe & S. R. Steinberg (Eds.), *Conterpoints: Studies in postmodern theory of education* (Vol. 223). New York, NY: Peter Lang.

Mansfiend, N. (2000). *Subjectivity: Theories of the self from Freud to Haraway.* New York, NY: New York University Press.

Marcuse, H. (1964). *One-dimensional man: Studies in the ideology of advanced industrial society.* Boston, MA: Beacon Press.

Marple, H. D. (1975). *The world of music.* Boston, MA: Allyn and Bacon.

Martin, R. (2002). *Financialization of daily life.* Philadelphia, PA: Temple University Press.

Martinez, T. A. (1997). Popular culture as oppositional culture: Rap as resistance. *Sociological Perspectives, 40*(2), 265–286.

Mayo, P. (2013). The Gramscian influence. In R. Lake & T. Kress (Eds.), *Paulo Freire's intellectual roots: Towards historicity in praxis* (pp. 53–64). New York, NY: Bloomsbury.

McCarthy, M., & Goble, J. S. (2002). Music education philosophy: Changing times. *Music Educators Journal, 89*, 19–26.

McLaren, P. (1995). *Critical pedagogy and predatory culture.* New York, NY: Routledge.

McLaren, P. (1998). *Life in schools: An introduction to critical pedagogy in the foundations of education.* New York, NY: Longman.

McLaren, P., & Kincheloe, J. (Eds.). (2007). Critical pedagogy: Where are we now? In J. L. Kincheloe & S. R. Steinberg (Eds.), *Counterpoints: Studies in the postmodern theory of education* (Vol. 299). New York, NY: Peter Lang.

Merriam, A. P. (1964). *The anthropology of music.* Evanston, IL: Northwestern University Press.

Mignolo, W. D. (2000). *Local histories/global designs: Coloniality, subaltern knowledges, and border thinking.* Princeton, NJ: Princeton University Press.

Mignolo, W. D. (2011). *The darker side of western modernity: Global futures, decolonial options.* Durham, NC: Duke University Press.

Milnes, G. (1999). *Play of a fiddle.* Lexington, KY: The University Press of Kentucky.

Minissale, G. (2009). *Framing consciousness in art: Transcultural perspectives.* New York, NY: Rodopi.

Mitchell, T. (Ed.). (2001). *Global noise: Rap and hip-hop outside the USA.* Middletown, CT: Wesleyan University Press.

Moeller, H-G. (2006). *Luhmann explained: From souls to systems.* Chicago, IL: Open Court.

Nattiez, J. (1990). *Music and discourse: Toward a semiology of music.* Princeton, NJ: Princeton University Press.

Neal, L. (1968). The Black arts movement. *The Drama Review: TDR, 12*(4), 28–39.

Neal, M. A. (2002). *Soul babies: Black popular culture and the post-soul aesthetic.* New York, NY: Routledge.

Noffke, S. E., & Somekh, B. (2009) *The sage handbook of educational action research.* London: Sage Press.

Perlman, M. (1998). The social meanings of modal practices: Status, gender, history, and pathet in Central Javanese music. *Ethnomusicology, 42*(1), 45–80.

Pinar, W. F. (2010). Foreword. In J. A. Brian, D. Schultz Sandlin, & J. Burdick (Eds.), *Handbook of public pedagogy.* New York, NY: Routledge.

Plato. (2000). *The republic* (B. Jowett, Trans.). New York, NY: Dover.

Poster, M. (1979). Semiology and critical theory: From Marx to Baudrillard. In *The problems of reading in contemporary American criticism: A symposium* (Autumn), 275–288.

Qureshi, R. B. (2000). Confronting the social: Mode of production and the sublime for (Indian) art music. *Ethnomusicology, 44*(1), 15–38.

Rancière, J. (1991). *The ignorant schoolmaster: Five lessons in intellectual emancipation*. Stanford, CA: Stanford University Press.

Rancière, J. (2000). What aesthetics can mean (B. Holmes, Trans.). In P. Osborne (Ed.), *From an aesthetic point of view: Philosophy, art, and the senses*. London, UK: Serpent's Tail.

Rancière, J. (2005). From politics to aesthetics? *Paragraph, 28*(1), 13–25.

Rancière, J. (2007). *The politics of aesthetics: The distribution of the sensible* (G. Rockhill, Trans.). London, UK: Continuum.

Rancière, J. (2010). *Dissensus: On politics and aesthetics*. New York, NY: Continuum.

Regelski, T. A. (1996). Prolegomenon to a paraxial philosophy of music and music education. *Musiikkikasvatus: The Finnish Journal of Music Education, 1*(1), 24.

Regelski. T. A. (2011). Praxialism and 'aesthetic this, aesthetic that, aesthetic whatever.' *Action, Criticism, and Theory for Music Education, 10*(2), 61–100.

Rice, T. (2004). *Music in Bulgaria, experiencing music, expressing culture*. New York, NY: Oxford University Press.

Robson, M. (2005). Jacques Rancière aesthetic communities. *Paragraph, 28*(1), 77–95.

Rose, T. (1994). *Black noise: Rap music and Black culture in contemporary America*. Hanover: Wesleyan University Press.

Roy, K. (2003). Teachers in nomadic spaces: Deleuze and curriculum. In W. F. Pinar (Ed.), *Complicated conversation*. New York, NY: Peter Lang.

Sandlin, J. A., Schultz, B. D., & Burdick, J. (2010). Understanding, mapping, and exploring the terrain of public pedagogy. In J. A. Sandlin, B. D. Schultz, & J. Burdick (Eds.), *Handbook of public pedagogy*. New York, NY: Routledge.

Schiller, F. (1954). *On the aesthetic education of man*. Mineola, NY: Dover Publications.

Schloss, J. G. (2009). *Foundation: B-boys, b-girls, and hip-hop culture in New York*. New York, NY: Oxford University Press.

Seeger, A. (2004). *Why Suyá sing: A musical anthropology of an Amazonian people*. Chicago, IL: University of Illinois Press.

Shepherd, J. (1991). *Music as social text*. Cambridge, UK: Polity Press.

Sipress, J. M., & Voelker, D. J. (2011). The end of the history survey course: The rise and fall of the coverage model. *The Journal of American History, 97*(4), 1050–1066.

Small, C. (1998). *Musicking: The meanings of performing and listening*. Hanover, NH: Wesleyan University Press.

Smethurst, J. (2003). 'Pat your foot and turn the corner': Amiri Baraka, the Black arts movement, and the poetics of a popular avant-garde. *African American Review, 37*(2–3), 261–270.

Spivak, G. C. (2012). *An aesthetic education in the era of globalization*. Cambridge, MA: Harvard University Press.

Steigler, B. (2010). *Taking care of youth and the generations*. Stanford, CA: Stanford University Press.

Steinberg, S. R. (2001). *Multi/intercultural conversations: A reader*. New York, NY: Peter Lang.

Steinberg, S. R. (2009). *Diversity and multiculturalism: A reader*. New York, NY: Peter Lang.

Stinson, S. W. (1998). Maxine Greene and arts education. In W. F. Pinar (Ed.), *The passionate mind of Maxine Greene* (pp. 221–228). New York, NY: Routledge.

Stovall, D. (2010). A note on the politics of place and public pedagogy: Critical race theory, schools, community, and social justice. In J. A. Sandlin, B. D. Schultz., & J. Burdick (Eds.), *Handbook of public pedagogy*. New York, NY: Routledge.

Sullivan, R. E. (2003). Rap and race: It's got a nice beat, but what about the message? *Journal of Black Studies, 33*(5), 605–622.

Swonger, M. (2006). Foucault and the hupomnemata: Self writing as an art of life. *Senior Honors Project* (Paper 18).

Tagg, P. (1987). Musicology and the semiotics of popular music. *Semiotica, 66*(1/3), 279–298.

Tagg, P. (1992). Towards a sign typology of music. In R. Dalmonte & M. Baroni (Eds.), *Secondo convegno europeo di analisi musicale* (pp. 369–378). Trento, Italy: Università degli studi di Trento.

Tagg, P. (2012, forthcoming). *Music's Meaning; provisional version*. Retrieved from www.tagg.org/mmmsp/NonMuso.pdf

REFERENCES

Thomas, J. W. (2000). *A review of research on project-based learning*. Report prepared for The Autodesk Foundation. Retrieved May 18, 2009, from http://www.bie.org/index.php/site/RE/pbl_research/29

Tuhiwai Smith, L. (2012). *Decolonizing methodologies: Research and Indigenous peoples*. New York, NY: Zed Books.

Turino, T. (1989). The coherence of social style and music creation among the Aymara in Southern Peru. *Ethnomusicology, 33*(1), 1–30.

Wasiak. E. (2013). *Teaching instrumental music in Canadian schools*. Toronto, ON: Oxford University Press.

Waterman, C. A. (1990). *Jùjú: A social history and ethnography of an African popular music*. Chicago, IL: The University of Chicago Press.

Werner, C. H. (1994). *Playing the changes: From Afro-modernism to the jazz impulse*. Urbana, IL: University of Illinois Press.

Westerlund, H. (2003). Reconsidering aesthetic experience in praxial music education. *Philosophy of Music Education Review, 11*(1), 45–62.

Williams, A. D. (2009). The critical cultural cypher: Remaking Paulo Freire's cultural circles using Hip Hop culture. *International Journal of Critical Pedagogy, 2*(1), 1–29.

Williams, L. (2010). Hip-hop as a site of public pedagogy. In J. A. Sandlin, B. D. Schultz, & J. Burdick (Eds.), *Handbook of public pedagogy: Education and learning beyond schooling* (pp. 221–232). New York, NY: Routledge.

Williams, R. (1980). *Culture and materialism*. New York, NY: Verso.

Willison, J., & O'Reagen, K. (2007). Commonly known, commonly not known, totally unknown: a framework for students becoming researchers. *Higher Education Research & Development, 26*(4), 393–409.

Wise, T. (2010). *Color-blind: The rise of post-racial politics and the retreat from racial equity*. San Francisco, CA: City Lights Books.

Wright, H. K. (2003). Cultural studies as praxis: (Making) an autobiographical case. *Cultural Studies, 17*(6), 805–822.

CPSIA information can be obtained
at www.ICGtesting.com
Printed in the USA
LVOW04s0749061216
516012LV00001B/1/P